Best Poems of 1969

Best Poems of 1969
Borestone Mountain
Poetry Awards 1970

(Standford, Calif.)

A Compilation of Original Poetry
Published in Magazines of the
English-speaking World in 1969

Twenty-second Annual Issue
Volume XXII

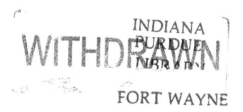
Pacific Books, Publishers, Palo Alto, California
1970

ISBN: 0-87015-186-X.
Library of Congress Catalog Card No. 49-49262.

Printed and bound in the United States of America.

PACIFIC BOOKS, PUBLISHERS
P.O. Box 558, Palo Alto, California 94302

FOREWORD

Best Poems of 1969 presents a selection of poems first published in the year 1969 in magazines of the English-speaking world. The publications from which these poems were selected are listed in the "Contents." The subsequent reprintings and other recognitions are recorded under "Acknowledgments and Notes."

This is the twenty-second volume of the Borestone Mountain Poetry Awards series. With two variations in titles, the annual selections have been published each year beginning with the first volume, *Poetry Awards 1949*. The title of the fifth volume included the full name of the literary trust, *Borestone Mountain Poetry Awards 1953*, to avoid confusion with other "awards." The seventh volume identified the year of the selections, *Best Poems of 1955*, with the subtitle, *Borestone Mountain Poetry Awards 1956*, which continued the sequence of earlier titles. The few requirements established for the selections of the first volume have never been changed. A poem is eligible if it is the first printing and not over one hundred lines. Translations, reprints, and unpublished poems are not considered.

The editorial procedure has also been consistent throughout the twenty-two years. Some three hundred or more poems are selected by the reading staff during a year. When the year's selections are complete, copies are sent to the judges with the names of the authors and periodicals deleted. The judges vote for their individual preferences and a tabulation of the scores determines the final selections. The highest scores are the winners of the year's awards.

This year "Children at Their Games" by Joan LaBombard received the first award of $300. "Everything" by Robin Skelton won the second award of $200, and "Plainsong for Everyone Who Was Killed Yesterday" by David Wagoner received the third award of $100.

The editors gratefully acknowledge permission to reprint these selected poems from the magazines, publishers, and authors owning the copyrights.

The Editors

ACKNOWLEDGMENTS AND NOTES

"The Parachutist" by Jon Anderson, selected from the first printing in the January 2, 1969 issue of *The New Yorker* is reprinted from *Death & Friends* by Jon Anderson, by permission of the University of Pittsburgh Press, copyright 1970 by Jon Anderson.

"Soonest Mended" by John Ashbery was first published in Issue No. 47, summer 1969 of *Paris Review*. Subsequently the poem was reprinted in *The Double Dream of Spring* by John Ashbery, copyright 1970 by John Ashbery, published by E. P. Dutton & Co., Inc. and reprinted with their permission.

"Natural Linguistics" by W. H. Auden is reprinted from the October 1969 issue of *Harper's Magazine* by permission of the author, copyright 1969, by Harper's Magazine, Inc.

"The Current" by Wendell Berry was originally selected from the first printing in Vol. XXII, No. 3, the autumn 1969 issue of *The Hudson Review*. "The Mad Farmer Revolution, Being a Fragment of the Natural History of New Eden, in Homage to Mr. Ed McClanahan, One of the Locals," also by Wendell Berry, was selected from the fall 1969 issue of *Southern Poetry Review*. The poem was also published in the fall issue of *Sequoia*, the student literary magazine of Stanford University. "The Current," copyright 1969 by Wendell Berry, is now reprinted from his volume *Farming: A Hand Book* by permission of Harcourt Brace Jovanovich, Inc. "The Mad Farmer Revolution, Being a Fragment of the Natural History of New Eden, in Homage to Mr. Ed McClanahan, One of the Locals," copyright 1970 by Wendell Berry, is also reprinted from his volume *Farming: A Hand Book* by permission of Harcourt Brace Jovanovich, Inc.

"The Stranding" by Philip Booth was first published in *The Hudson Review*, Vol. XXII, No. 2, summer 1969 issue. The poem is to be included in *Margins* by Philip Booth, copyright 1969 by Philip Booth, and is reprinted by permission of The Viking Press, Inc.

"A Double Haunting" by Bruce Dawe, selected from the original printing in *Poetry Magazine* (Australia), was included in his fourth book *Beyond the Subdivisions*, published in Novem-

CONTENTS

Joan LaBombard: (*First Award*)
Children at Their Games   1
The Virginia Quarterly Review—Summer
Robin Skelton: (*Second Award*)   Everything   3
Poetry Northwest—Winter
David Wagoner: (*Third Award*)
Plainsong for Everyone Who Was Killed Yesterday   5
The New Yorker—February 15
Linda Allardt: Singers   8
Poetry Northwest—Summer
Jon Anderson: The Parachutist   9
The New Yorker—January 2
John Ashbery: Soonest Mended   11
The Paris Review—No. 47, Summer
W. H. Auden: Moon Landing   14
The New Yorker—September 6
W. H. Auden: Natural Linguistics   16
Harper's Magazine—October
Donald W. Baker: The Snapshot   18
Southern Poetry Review—Spring
Wendell Berry: The Current   20
The Hudson Review—Vol. XXII, No. 3, Autumn
Wendell Berry: The Mad Farmer Revolution, Being a
Fragment of the Natural History of New Eden, in
Homage to Mr. Ed McClanahan, One of the Locals   21
Southern Poetry Review—Fall
Alison J. Bielski: Second Genesis   23
Anglo-Welsh Review (Wales)—Winter
Philip Booth: Let the Trees   27
Poetry Northwest—Autumn
Philip Booth: The Stranding   30
The Hudson Review—Vol. XXII, No. 2, Summer

Michael Dennis Browne: News from the House   32
                    The New Yorker—January 2
Hayden Carruth: Emergency Haying   36
            The Virginia Quarterly Review—Spring
Larry Clarke: Morning Walk   39
                        South—Vol. 1, No. 1
David M. Collins: Three Poems   42
                        Epos—Spring
Jeni Couzyn: The Red Hen's Last Will and Testament
                    to the Last Cock on Earth   43
                    Ambit (England)—No. 41
Jack Crawford, Jr.:   Sideshow   45
    The Fiddlehead (Canada)—November-December
John Creighton: Green Hides: Lines to a Pale Lady   48
                    The Outsider—Nos. 4 & 5
Bruce Dawe: A Double Haunting   52
                Poetry Magazine (Australia)—June
Rick DeMarinis: Fan Letter to Glenn Ford   53
                Poetry Northwest—Winter 1968-69
Sonya Dorman: Passed a Swan   56
                Saturday Review—January 18
Charles Edward Eaton: Squashes   57
            Canadian Forum (Canada)—June
David Allan Evans: A Jumper   59
                Shenandoah—Autumn
Joan Finnigan: For Himself in the Spring*   60
                Quarry (Canada)—Fall
Robin Fulton: Music of the Spheres   62
            Outposts (England)—Summer
Arthur Gregor: Worldliness   64
                The New Republic—April 26
S. Gresser: Poem for John Bradley   65
                Illuminations—No. 4
Michael Hamburger: Travelling   67
                Outsider—Nos. 4 & 5

Gwen Harwood: Father and Child   70
        Quadrant (Australia)—March-April
C. David Heymann: Spanish Soldier   73
        The Smith—Special Issue 1
David Holbrook: Dead Duck   75
        Workshop (England)—No. 7
David Holbrook: Whipsnade   77
        Workshop (England)—No. 6
A. D. Hope: The School of Night   79
        Poetry—June
Josephine Jacobsen: My Small Aunt   81
        The Kenyon Review—Issue 1
Shirley Kaufman: It Stays   83
        The Southern Review—Spring
Arnold Kenseth: Bird, Fox, and I   85
        The Virginia Quarterly Review—Summer
Arnold Kenseth: Summer Student   87
        The Virginia Quarterly Review—Summer
Timothy Kidd: Derelict Freehold   88
        The Poetry Review (England)—Autumn
James Kirkup: A Garland for Emily   90
        Poetry Australia—August
Carolyn Kizer: The Dying Goddess   93
        The New Republic—April 19
Maxine Kumin: The Presence   95
        Harper's Magazine—December
Philip Legler: On Receiving a Drawing of Your Hand   96
        Perspective—Autumn
Laurence Lerner: Adam Names the Creatures   99
        Outposts (England)—Spring
Christopher Levenson: The Burglar   101
        The Canadian Forum (Canada)—August
C. Day Lewis: Golden Age: Monart, Co. Wexford   103
        Outposts (England)—Spring
Herbert Lomas: Judas Speaks   104
        The London Magazine (England)—February

Edward Lucie-Smith: At Midnight   107
                The Southern Review—Summer
Roy MacGregor-Hastie: Tam Rating   108
                The Poetry Review (England)—Winter
Wes Magee: Postcard from a Long Way Off   109
                The Poetry Review (England)—Autumn
Howard McCord: My Cow   110
                New Mexico Quarterly—Winter-Spring
William Meredith: Effort at Speech   111
                The New Yorker—December 6
William Meredith:
                Waking Dream About a Lost Child   113
                        The New Yorker—July 12
Leonard Nathan: In Defense of the Makers   115
        Quarterly Review of Literature—Vol. 26, No. 1-2
A. Poulin, Jr.:   The Dream   116
                The Atlantic Monthly—April
Lawrence Raab: The Hero on His Way Home   118
        The American Scholar—Vol. 38, No. 3, Summer
Lawrence Raab: Walking Alone   120
                        Poetry—February
Denise Salfeld: Spring   121
                The Poetry Review (England)—Spring
Peter Scupham: Family Ties   123
                The Poetry Review (England)—Summer
Richard Shelton: The Crossing   124
                The Outsider—Nos. 4 & 5
Glen Siebrasse: The Alburg Auction, Vermont   126
                The Canadian Forum (Canada)—March
Helen Singer: The Unguarded Rooms   128
                        Poetry—January
Tom Smith: Birthday in Sabula   130
                        Foxfire—Winter
Ann Stanford: The Cocks   132
                Prairie Schooner—Summer

Ann Stanford: The Descent 133
                    The Southern Review—Spring
Ann Stanford: The Organization of Space 135
                       Prairie Schooner—Summer
Karen Swenson: Farewell to Fargo: Selling the House 137
                        The New Yorker—October 18
May Swenson: I Look at My Hand 140
                     The Southern Review—Winter
Evelyn Thorne: Tonight 141
                           Epos—Summer
Charles Tomlinson: Assassin 143
          The London Magazine (England)—October
James Turner: Suffolk Stallion 145
             The Poetry Review (England)—Spring
Robert Penn Warren: Lyrics from *Audubon: A Vision* 146
                 The Yale Review—Vol. LIX, October
Reed Whittemore: The Winter of Our Discontent 148
                    The New Republic—March 1
Richard Wilbur: The Agent 149
     Quarterly Review of Literature—Vol. 26, No. 1-2
Richard Wilbur: For Dudley 152
                     The Hudson Review—Winter
Peter Wild: Sunday Breweryworks 154
                           Spirit—Summer
Robley Wilson, Jr.:   The Immortalist 156
                  The Atlantic Monthly—November
John Woods: The Sleepwalker 158
                     Poetry Northwest—Autumn

*Variation in title since original publication. See acknowledgments.

Best Poems of 1969

CHILDREN AT THEIR GAMES

They are at home in air and water
And in the long grass, murmurous with sound,
They glide as confidently as snakes
Between the blind worm and the fiddling cricket.
From the kingdom of their skins,
They put forth light antennae and become
The quail's egg and the hare's heartbeat.
They are a listening instrument, an ear,
A mouth for the grasshopper,
And sensuous as the sun,
They harbor the uncombed meadow in their blood.

We have lost the sense of it;
Of the littered nest, the twigs, the torn breast-fur.
The horned snail's silver track befouls our sight.
The sea wave lifts to our unknowing
Bearing the fisher child;
But these,
Sleek-headed as the otters, taste of salt,
Of the long wave and the sun, the rank sea-smell.
They teach the rainbow schools
Of bass and porpoise a glittering artistry,
At ease in the shell of self a wave foists up.

We have lost the sense of air, the textured lightness
In which the bare bones flower.
Their knowing is the knowing of hawks, of finches,
Of the hummingbird's delicate balance
Over the fuchsia's bell.
They are at home in the bodies of themselves.
In the wren's nest, in the grass, in tumbling rivers,
They touch the sleeping source
Of the blind mole's slow contentment, the ease
Of lazing trout in shallows,
And with the larks,
Exploded like small rockets toward the sun,
They fathom the light of morning in their bones.

JOAN LABOMBARD

EVERYTHING

Everything is, in the light of everything, holy.
But do not expect a catalogue of grace,
trees, leaves, grass, and children suddenly shouting
Hi-Hi, loudly, running in their playground,
for to select is always to leave out something
quiet, unnoticed, like the snail shell lying
under the black and rotten bit of the gatepost,
or the swing of the signature on the paper,
all of a movement. Everything is moving
in its own direction, sure as owls
dipping the blind hedges, the small stone walls
in the stiff hills where everything keeps house
within the sound of wind, each, any, stirring
slowly towards itself, defeat and conquest,
end and beginning, meaningless, arrival
only a word to stand for somewhere else
imbued with what we are more than ourselves.
And this we must remember: every thing
is, before everything, holy and astir
with an unfolding plentitude we are
the heirs of and bequeathers to our sons.
Therefore, be thankful when you thank, be sure
when time assures you on the dragging path,
be kind when you are kindred, do not lend
uncertainties to strangers, or take truth
away from anyone, but still be still
in movement and in peace, the turning word
always upon your silence. Look about.

Everything, before everything, is yours,
and none an island—no, none, none, not one
but is the others'. We possess ourselves
only so far as others lean to us,
and draw us, moving, into their stirred house,
as easily as air, only so far
as everything remains itself and sings.

ROBIN SKELTON

PLAINSONG FOR EVERYONE WHO
WAS KILLED YESTERDAY

You haven't missed anything yet:
One dawn, one breakfast, and a little weather,
The clamor of birds whose names
You didn't know, perhaps some housework,
Homework, or a quick sale.
The trees are still the same color
And the Mayor is still the mayor, and we're not
Having anything unusual for lunch.
No one has kissed her yet
Or slept with him. Our humdrum lives
Have gone on humming and drumming
Through one more morning.

But, for a while, we must consider
What you might have wished
To do or look like. So far,
Thinking of you, no one has forgotten
Anything he wanted to remember.
Your death is fresh as a prize
Vegetable—familiar but amazing,
Admirable but not yet useful—
And you're in a class
By yourself. We don't know
Quite what to make of you.

You've noticed you don't die
All at once. Some people, like me,
Still offer you our songs
Because we don't know any better
And because you might believe
At last whatever we sing
About you, since no one else is dreaming
Of singing: *Remember that time*
When you were wrong? Well, you were right.
And here's more comfort. All fires burn out
As quickly as they burn. They're over
Before we know it, like accidents.

You may feel you were interrupted
Rudely, cut off in the middle
Of something crucial,
And you may even be right
Today, but tomorrow
No one will think so.
Today consists of millions
Of newsless current events
Like the millions of sticks and stones
From here to the horizon. What are you
Going to miss? The calendar
Is our only program.

Next week or next year
Is soon enough to consider
Those brief occasions you might rather
Not have lost—the strange ones
You might go so far
As to say you could have died for:
Love, for example, or all
The other inflammations of the cerebral
Cortex, the astounding, irreversible
Moments you kept promising yourself
To honor, which are as far away
Now as they ever were.

DAVID WAGONER

SINGERS

Let now and then a line
sing, if only to underscore
the stripped sense of thing.

Lord, we are pruned to the core
but a bird will be
sassy in the stripped tree.

Lord, we are pared to the bone
but the bone is stubborn.
It talks back even to thee.

Bird, bone, thing—
Lord of our lessening,
can you hear us sing?

LINDA ALLARDT

THE PARACHUTIST

Then the air was perfect. And his descent
to the white earth slowed.
                    Falling
became an ability to rest—as

the released breath
believes in life. Further down it snowed,

a confusion of slow novas
which his shoes touched upon, which seemed
as he fell by

to be rising. From every
small college and rural town:
    the clearest, iced blossoms of thought,

but gentle.
                    Then the housetops
of friends, who
he thought had been speaking of his arrival,
withdrew, each from another.

He saw that his friends
lived in a solitude they had not ever said aloud.

Strangely he thought this good.

    The world, in fact
which in these moments he came toward,

seemed casual.
Had he been thinking this all along?
  A life
where he belonged, having lived with himself

always, as a secret friend.

A few may have seen him then. In evidence:
the stopped dots
of children & dogs, sudden weave

    of a car—
acquaintances, circling up
into the adventure they imagined. They saw him drop

through the line breaks
and preciousness of art

down to the lake
which openly awaited him.
          Here the thin
 green ice allowed him in.

Some ran, and were late.
These would
forever imagine tragedy

(endless descent,
his face floating among the reeds,
unrecognized), as those

who imagine the silence of a guest
to be mysterious, or wrong.

JON ANDERSON

SOONEST MENDED

Barely tolerated, living on the margin
In our technological society, we were always having to be
      rescued
On the brink of destruction, like heroines in *Orlando Furioso*
Before it was time to start all over again.
There would be thunder in the bushes, a rustling of coils,
And Angelica, in the Ingres painting, was considering
The colorful but small monster near her toe, as though won-
      dering whether forgetting
The whole thing might not, in the end, be the only solution.
And then there always came a time when
Happy Hooligan in his rusted green automobile
Came plowing down the course, just to make sure everything
      was O.K.,
Only by that time we were in another chapter and confused
About how to receive this latest piece of information.
Was it information? Weren't we rather acting this out
For someone else's benefit, thoughts in a mind
With room enough and to spare for our little problems (so
      they began to seem),
Our daily quandary about food and the rent and bills to be
      paid?
To reduce all this to a small variant,
To step free at last, minuscule on the gigantic plateau—
This was our ambition: to be small and clear and free.
Alas, the summer's energy wanes quickly,
A moment and it is gone. And no longer
May we make the necessary arrangements, simple as they
      are.

Our star was brighter perhaps when it had water in it.
Now there is no question even of that, but only
Of holding on to the hard earth so as not to get thrown off,
With an occasional dream, a vision: a robin flies across
The upper corner of the window, you brush your hair away
And cannot quite see, or a wound will flash
Against the sweet faces of the others, something like:
This is what you wanted to hear, so why
Did you think of listening to something else? We are all talkers
It is true, but underneath the talk lies
The moving and not wanting to be moved, the loose
Meaning, untidy and simple like a threshing floor.

These then were some hazards of the course,
Yet though we knew the course *was* hazards and nothing else
It was still a shock when, almost a quarter of a century later,
The clarity of the rules dawned on you for the first time.
They were the players, and we who had struggled at the game
Were merely spectators, though subject to its vicissitudes
And moving with it out of the tearful stadium, borne on
    shoulders, at last.
Night after night this message returns, repeated
In the flickering bulbs of the sky, raised past us, taken away
    from us,
Yet ours over and over until the end that is past truth,
The being of our sentences, in the climate that fostered them,
Not ours to own, like a book, but to be with, and sometimes
To be without, alone and desperate.
But the fantasy makes it ours, a kind of fence-sitting
Raised to the level of an esthetic ideal. These were moments,
    years,
Solid with reality, faces, namable events, kisses, heroic acts,
But like the friendly beginning of a geometrical progression
Not too reassuring, as though meaning could be cast aside
    some day

When it had been outgrown. Better, you said, to stay cower-
    ing
Like this in the early lessons, since the promise of learning
Is a delusion, and I agreed, adding that
Tomorrow would alter the sense of what had already been
    learned,
That the learning process is extended in this way, so that from
    this standpoint
None of us ever graduates from college,
For time is an emulsion, and probably thinking not to grow up
Is the brightest kind of maturity for us, right now at any rate.
And you see, both of us were right, though nothing
Has somehow come to nothing: the avatars
Of our conforming to the rules and living
Around the home have made—well, in a sense, "good citizens"
    of us,
Brushing the teeth and all that, and learning to accept
The charity of the hard moments as they are doled out,
For this is action, this not being sure, this careless
Preparing, sowing the seeds crooked in the furrow,
Making ready to forget, and always coming back
To the mooring of starting out, that day so long ago.

JOHN ASHBERY

MOON LANDING

It's natural the Boys should whoop it up for
so huge a phallic triumph, an adventure
   it would not have occurred to women
   to think worthwhile, made possible only

because we like huddling in gangs and knowing
the exact time: yes, our sex may with reason
   hurrah the deed, although the motives
   that primed it were somewhat less than *menschlich*.

A grand gesture. But what does it period?
What does it osse? We were always adroiter
   with objects than lives and more facile
   at courage than kindness: from the moment

the first flint was flaked, this landing was merely
a matter of time. But our selves, like Adam's,
   still don't fit us exactly, modern
   only in this—our lack of decorum.

Homer's heroes were certainly no braver than
our Trio, but more fortunate: Hector
   was exused the insult of having
   his valor covered by television.

Worth *going* to see? I can well believe it.
Worth *seeing?* Mneh! I once rode through a desert
   and was not charmed: give me a watered
   lively garden, remote from blatherers

about the New, the von Brauns and their ilk, where
on August mornings I can count the morning
    glories, where to die has a meaning,
    and no engine can shift my perspective.

Unsmudged, thank God, my Moon still queens the Heavens
as She ebbs and fulls, a Presence to glop at,
    Her Old Man, made of grit not protein,
    still visits my Austrian several

with His old detachment, and the old warnings
still have power to scare me: Hybris comes to
    a nasty finish, Irreverence
    is a greater oaf than Superstition.

Our apparatniks will continue making
the usual squalid mess called History:
    all we can pray for is that artists,
    chefs and saints may still appear to blithe it.

W. H. AUDEN

16

NATURAL LINGUISTICS

for Peter Salus

Every created thing has ways of pronouncing its ownhood:
   basic and used by all, even the mineral tribes,
is the hieroglyphical *koine* of visual appearance
   which, though it lacks the verb, is, when compared with our own
heaviest lexicons so much richer and subtler in shape-nouns,
   color-adjectives and apt prepositions of place.
Verbs first appear with the flowers who issue imperative odors
   which, with their taste for sweets, insects are bound to obey:
motive, too, in the eyes of beasts is the language of gesture
   (urban life has, alas, sadly impoverished ours),
signals of interrogation, friendship, threat and appeasement,
   instantly taken in, seldom, if ever, misread.
All who have managed to break through the primal barrier of silence
   into an audible world find the indicative AM:
though some carnivores, leaving messages written in urine,
   use a preterite WAS, none can conceive of a WILL,
nor have they ever made subjunctive or negative statements,
   even cryptics whose lives hang upon telling a fib.
Rage and grief they can sing but not self-reproach or repentance,
   nor have they legends to tell, yet their respect for a rite
is more pious than ours, for a complex code of releasers
   trains them to walk in the ways which their ur-ancestors trod.
(Some of these codes remain mysteries to us: for instance,
   fish who travel in huge loveless anonymous turbs,
what is it keeps them in line? Our single certainty is that
   minnows deprived of their fore-brains go it gladly alone.)

Since in their circles it's not good form to say anything novel,
    none ever stutter on *er,* guddling in vain for a word,
none are at loss for an answer: none, it would seem, are bilingual
    but, if they cannot translate, that is the ransom they pay
for just doing their thing well, never attempting to publish
    all the world as we do into our picture at once.
If they have never laughed, at least they have never talked drivel,
    never tortured their own kind for a point of belief,
never, marching to war, inflamed by fortissimo music,
    hundreds of miles from home died for a verbal whereas.

"Dumb" we may call them but, surely, our poets are right in assuming
    all would prefer that they were rhetorized at than about.

                                              W. H. AUDEN

THE SNAPSHOT

Squinting against the sun,
her blowing hair a cloud across her eyes,
she kneels on sand

where white surf brims
her summer and a salt wind scatters
her cakes and castle.

What stranded child have I
lifted from the years that stiffen
in this yellowed shoebox?

Is it you, printed
on ebbing August afternoons
until the salt cakes

at your temples
and your stare alters with the sun?
Does the child cry

in your voice now,
touch me with your hands withered
in the brines of marriage?

Wife, in the mind's cheap
camera, where castle and cakes and child
lose the light,

the sea is lifting
in the flood that cracks and shadows all
our albumed beaches,

and a cold wind
chills the memory and scatters
all our summers.

Towards narrowing shores
my pulse is stumbling down the steep
dunes for a child,

for I would lift her up,
above collapsing sands, and show her
scallop shells.

But I can only make
this fading photograph of words for her,
for all her ruined castles.

DONALD W. BAKER

THE CURRENT

Having once put his hand into the ground,
seeding there what he hopes will outlast him,
a man has made a marriage with his place,
and if he leaves it his flesh will ache to go back.
His hand has given up its birdlife in the air.
It has reached into the dark like a root
and begun to wake, quick and mortal, in timelessness,
a flickering sap coursing upward into his head
so that he sees the old tribespeople bend
in the sun, digging with sticks, the forest opening
to receive their hills of corn, squash, and beans,
their lodges and graves, and closing again.
He is made their descendent, what they left
in the earth rising into him like a seasonal juice.
And he sees the bearers of his own blood arriving,
the forest burrowing into the earth as they come,
their hands gathering the stones up into walls,
and relaxing, the stones crawling back into the ground
to lie still under the black wheels of machines.
The current flowing to him through the earth
flows past him, and he sees one descended from him,
a young man who has reached into the ground,
his hand held in the dark as by a hand.

WENDELL BERRY

THE MAD FARMER REVOLUTION, BEING A FRAGMENT OF THE NATURAL HISTORY OF NEW EDEN, IN HOMAGE TO MR. ED McCLANAHAN, ONE OF THE LOCALS

The mad farmer, the thirsty one,
went dry. When he had time
he threw a visionary high
lonesome on the holy communion wine.
"It is an awesome event
when an earthen man has drunk
his fill of the blood of a god,"
people said, and got out of his way.
He plowed the churchyard, the
minister's wife, three graveyards
and a golf course. In a parking lot
he planted a forest of little pines.
He sanctified the groves,
dancing at night in the oak shades
with goddesses. He led
a field of corn to creep up
and tassel like an Indian tribe
on the court house lawn. Pumpkins
ran out to the ends of their vines
to follow him. Ripe plums
and peaches reached into his pockets.
Flowers sprang up in his tracks
everywhere he stepped. And then
his planter's eye fell on
that parson's fair fine lady
again. "O holy plowman," cried she,
"I am all grown up in weeds.
Pray, bring me back into good tilth."

He tilled her carefully
and laid her by, and she
did bring forth others of her kind,
and others, and some more.
They sowed and reaped till all
the countryside was filled
with farmers and their brides sowing
and reaping. When they died
they became two spirits of the woods.

On their graves were written
these words without sound:
"Here lies Saint Plowman.
Here lies Saint Fertile Ground."

WENDELL BERRY

SECOND GENESIS

I

We were warned to leave for the mountain,
pack up possessions and all the food
we could carry, to start in two days
for this special place, this bitter hill,
its ragged boulders, cliffs, green forests.
We listened to careful instructions
in our skyscraper flats, glass-fronted
office blocks, withdrew in orderly
fashion, camped in those fern-lined caverns.

It all seemed rather ridiculous,
leaving our modern civilisation
for this primitive mountain shelter,
but we knew we had to obey these
orders implicitly. Almost a week
passed, while we waited, observed from our
high safe shelter; then they began,
slow stuttering earthquakes, wave after wave
sweeping each hemisphere, every city
shaking, tumbling, disappearing
under cavernous clay. We watched in
horror from damp hide-outs, as our own
town finally shuddered, cracked, toppled

into yawning limestone jaws, those
beautiful broken buildings, roads,
library, shops, garages, all
falling like children's brick-balanced
towers into the land's hungry
gullet. Crouching together, past fear,
we survived in our primitive camp,
then came the startling realisation,
vast terrible emptiness. We were
alone, entirely alone, one chosen
unit saved from annihilation.

II

Later, courageously looking down
into that gaping crevasse, small
sudden movement fluttered, fresh
new beauty emerged, green spreading
plants furring derelict rubble,
bursting over bricks, while thin young
saplings sprouted between jagged
crags, fruiting in a whirling
of seasons, and a million
brilliant flowers spilt over
sombre rock. All across this broken
bleeding land, a vivid rainbow arched
curved petals, stems, creepers, sap-hissing
grass blades, a new fruitful Eden
covered smoking ruins, beckoned
us from our tangled hiding-place.

Cautiously, we clambered over oozing mud,
soft soil, loam, new grass. It was finished,
the horror, screaming, mass destruction.
We ran bewildered across fertile orchards,
knowing that we should live off the land,
nomadic as ancestors who toiled
ploughing, tilling, planting, reaping their
crops, making tents, tools, clothing. Reborn
from turmoil, this was our second chance.

III

This strange new birth, this turning-point,
this challenge became our accepted way
of life. We were calmer, more self-possessed,
independent and laughed freely.
Our sanity had returned. We had pushed
progress as far as we could endure it;
now there was only basic existence,
a handful of people breeding children,
finding food, living, dying, this
rough cruel life, yet we were happier
than we had ever been before.
But where was the flaw, that lurking
leaf-rolled worm, fat canker gnawing one
flamboyant rose? Lurking serpent-like in
our surroundings, or hidden in ourselves?
Would we rebuild our history,
start to destroy ourselves again?
Was the angel at the gate laughing
behind his white hand, or tolerant,
standing at ease with sheathed cold sword?

We made the mountain a sanctuary,
a place of pilgrimage for our people,
and often visited damp fern-lined caves,
stroking rough bark of forest trees, where our
terrified fingers had once torn splinters.
So we controlled our lonely kingdom
and prospered, but received no further
instructions, finding neither angel
nor sliding serpent, and continued
to work out our hidden destiny:

this was our hope, our second genesis.

ALISON J. BIELSKI

LET THE TREES

Let the trees be full.
                              Full,
you ask, for God's sake of *what?*
Leaves in due season, or snow;
a moon, if it comes to that.
Or, lacking as much, a night
after clouds full of wind.
                              What
do you mean you don't know
what I mean? Get out
of the house and into
the trees. You, through
fall-out and smoke, who
for six gravid days
have program'd yourselves
into space, tracking
your progress through
wave-lengths converged
on hundreds of lenses. . . .

It's no great matter what
starlings have already
flown, or stiffly still wait
in the branches; the seeds,
from their warm apogee,
have spun toward hard
re-entry. Refusing
how winter answers
your doubt, you might
even want, toward new
growth, to kneel at the root
of what you look up at.
Look, I say, to the trees,
and let your two eyes
fill them, even as then
your own two eyes may
be filled.
     We've looked
long enough at ourselves:
for six brave days without
love, computing cold pride
through a hundred lenses.
Proud of voyage less than
return, we've left no
hero in space; nor is
there a tree on the moon,
to feast on or look up to.

The computers whirr and blaze
in their own trajectory,
plotting how men return
to Texas to tell their story
to punchcards. Conditioned
to die, we watch ourselves
orbit on padded couches, banking
on tapes to program our
last defenses.
          Look
out the window, you
who have planted a tree
in your yard, or live
on the edge of a hedgerow;
you, whom computers have
fired, and gravity finally
tugged home: I pray you,
come to your senses.

PHILIP BOOTH

THE STRANDING

When I put my eyes up to
the eyes of my skull and
look in through both eyes

at once, out beyond shoals
of porpoises that sport
as if they'd been whelped in

my inner ear, all I can see
is myself at infinite
focus: a man the tide caught

on that same tidal ledge
where all his life
he has gathered kelp.

I can barely make out
his blue jacket and seaboots.
The tide is still coming.

His skiff is already gone.
It's already gotten dark
at the top of my skull;

through cracks in that sky
the Northern birds are homing.
Wreaths of kelp float up

through the bedrock; if I
weren't stranded so far
from myself, or if

the wind veered, I might try
to yell his name. But he's
already begun to listen

to how, as they whistle
and roll to breathe,
the porpoises click for sea room.

PHILIP BOOTH

NEWS FROM THE HOUSE

Love, I have warmed the car,
the snow between us lies

shaking at the sound of my wheels
pawing the ground, my radio

snorting through its shimmering
nostrils.
                    I

have command of the seats,
the trunk has been blessed

by Eskimos, and the hood
(or British Bonnet) anointed
with a stern steam.
                           There

is no time like the present,
send for me.

              Love, over
what dark miles do I come, shall I,
dark

as the wind round the house
I lie in,

the great bed, the long
night draining me,
                      Love,
in what season may it, tell me
the green date mice may

swear by, and the vast
branches spread dizzy those
distances my eyes too well

see through this winter. What
I have done that you

weep, what you have
worked that I
pace continually

this most sad house, meals
of its emptiness in every
corner, that the wind
                    sounds,

the house refusing to be musical,

in the sheerest dark. Tell me
the previous times, hear my

greed for you. Under it all
and the cold ground
                    we
sleeping you said, and ending,
the April waking, that trap
sprung.
        Love, in my
solitude my hands
garrisoned, hear them

nightly beside me muttering
of freedoms they were

warm in. How
on these nights the house
refusing to be musical
                    I

lie stone, seed-
cold, kernel of this

husked house, the white
miles between us

coiled soft as roads inside
me, my walls the blood
of rabbits, the bathroom
                    a lodge for hunters,
the bath

of fur and stained.
                    Love,

in what season, tell
me, I may unwrap this house
from me, these walls

remove, from my pockets
these stairs, drink

such dark no more
                    nor wear ever

this most sad hat of shadows. Tell

me, make me instructions,
send them like news
from a dairy.   I will feed

no more on this print and milk,
wait, crouch, mad in the sad house

refusing to be musical,
though I sing it each night the notes
my longest body is learning.

MICHAEL DENNIS BROWNE

EMERGENCY HAYING

Coming home with the last load I ride standing
on the tongue of the trailer behind the tractor
in its hot exhaust, lank with sweat in the strong

September sun with my arms strung out
awkwardly along the hayrack, cruciform.
Near five hundred bales we've put up this

afternoon, Marshall and I, and I feel it.
It makes me think of another who hung
like this on another cross. My hands are torn

by baling twine, not nails, and my side is pierced
by my ulcer, not a lance. The acid in my throat
is only hayseed. Yet exhaustion and the way

my body hangs from twisted shoulders, making
two cords that tie me on knots of pain
in the rising monoxide, recall that greater

suffering. Well, I change grip and the image
fades. It's been an unlucky summer. Heavy rains
brought on the grass tremendously, a monster crop,

but wet, always wet. Haying was long delayed.
Now this is the last chance to bring in
the winter's feed, and Marshall needs help.

We cut, rake, bale, and draw the bales
to the barn, these late, half-green,
improperly cured bales; some of them weigh

150 pounds, yet must be lugged by the twine
to the trailer, tossed up on the load, and then
at the barn unloaded on the conveyor

and distributed in the mow. I help, trying
my best, the desk-servant, word-worker,
and hold up my end pretty well too; but ah—

the close of day, how I fall down then.
My hands are sore, they flinch
when I light my pipe. I think of those

who have done slave labor, less able and
less well prepared than I. My wife
in the rye fields of Saxony, her father

in the camps of Moldavia and the Crimea,
and all clerks and housekeepers herded
to the great fields of torture. Hands

too bloodied cannot bear
even the touch of air, even
the touch of love. I have a friend

whose grandmother cut cane with a machete
and cut and cut, until one day
she snicked her hand off and took it

and threw it grandly at the sky. Now
in September our New England mountains
under a clear sky for which we're thankful at last

begin to glow, the maples, beeches, birches
assuming their first color. I look
beyond our famous hayfields to our famous hills,

to the notch where the sunset is beginning,
then in the other direction, eastward,
where a new-risen moon like a pale medallion

hangs in a lavender cloud beyond the barn.
My eyes sting with sweat and beauty. Who
is the Christ now, who

if not I? It must be so. My strength
is certain. And I stand up high
on the wagon tongue in my whole bones to say

woe to you, watch out
you sons-of-bitches who would drive men and women
to fields where they can only die.

HAYDEN CARRUTH

MORNING WALK

Ancient as air
I nose with dawn into the aging street,
into a crowd of used buildings
slacking their hold on things like old men.

Fresh from dreams I can't remember but
know were good, I wander,
wanting again to touch the bright flank of the world.
I move by silent buildings like
a pike in deep water, feeling
through my flesh the fineness
of grey dust, the thickness of brick.
In the dirt of old windows
the knives, statues, and sad jewelry
wait for the broken stares day will bring them.
Someone's barber pole starts.
A tobacco-store man sets newspapers
by a gutter stained with the spit of men long dead,
and on the ledges swallows gather like opera fans.
A blank man in suspenders sweeps yesterday's butts
from their sidewalk bed.
The first workers grub breakfast in the cafes.

All this is somehow like a belly laugh.
The smell of someone's cigar finds me
and memory, like a knife, slips in—
I'm five, on a Saturday morning walk with Pop,
gawking at the streets of Washington like
they were Atlantis.
The wise giant, puffing happily and
glowing in his wisdom, holds my hand,
casually explaining wonders.
I see a man with a doughnut cart
and know I'll eat all I want.

The moment passes like a flicked light
and others crowd in—
Waiting in the front yard, a cold Virginia dusk about me,
for him to come home from work;
playing with our black cat together;
listening to him tell a story from
his big chair, mother smiling from her kitchen.

I've found myself several people since then,
and years ago walked out on
that man and that boy.
The giant is growing grey now
and turning into an intense silent worker.
Evenings he tends his garden,
cold disappointment in me
lying on him like a spider.
We have descended to being friends,

but keep meeting each other in
joys we thought were private.
All his faces before me,
I can only turn away, turn
to the old dawning street, its brokenness
steeped in such things,
tramped by how many lost fathers and sons?

Here the ignorant pigeons still strut.
Cigarette packs in windows
are innocent as fifty years ago.
Weary or curious, the unending faces cruise by,
each accepting, for its own reasons, another dawn.

What can I do but forsake rising tears
and laugh with the tall giant of light holding
this ancient agile street
in its lap like a child?

LARRY CLARKE

THREE POEMS

WINTER

Before dawn, Tei Ch'i went into the garden.
The blue heron was far to the south.
The locust tree was naked and gray.
The water buffalo walked on ice.
On the sharp edge of morning
Tei Ch'i cut his fingers.

THE BELL

The sparrow takes the thorn out of the paw of the tiger.
The water buffalo guards the paths of the mountain.
The abbot says to Tei Ch'i,
"Call the monks to supper."
Tei Ch'i raises the hammer
To strike the great bell of the monastery.
Overhead, the blue heron flies north on sturdy wings.

THE QUESTION

The water buffalo brought Tei Ch'i a question.
"But I do not know the answer," said Tei Ch'i.
"Oh," said the water buffalo,
"This question is not to be answered.
"I brought it to you because I have no room."

Tei Ch'i took the question into the garden
And planted it beside the hyacinth.

DAVID M. COLLINS

THE RED HEN'S LAST WILL AND TESTAMENT TO THE LAST COCK ON EARTH

Mr Cockatoo I'm through.
        You
can take your splendid
reasoning and quick
precision and elegant
vision somewhere
else.
    You can take your
fine red comb and fast
feathered sex and high
concepts somewhere
else.
    Your race can take its
good influence and careful
words and strong wings and
bright eyes some other
place.
    You may be the
last manifestation but
you're not worth it.
            Now
that there's artificial
insemination since the
evolution of the cock

as a different species
you may as well wither
too.
    Hens need something
else. You make us feel
abandoned. You make us
feel like a place cocks
pop into. We stay in the
place alone.
        We await your
visitation. You pop in and
pop out. When we wake up
in the morning it is
silent.

    All the hens in the
farmyard feel exactly as
I do about you. We have
decided to quit.
        You all
can take off on your
massive Coxes High Powered
Jet Propelled
wings.
    We hens will stay here
laying our eggs in the
warm straw, dreaming of
foxes.

JENI COUZYN

SIDESHOW

I don't want to lie in a grave!
My bones with my name on them.
Cut in stone. Hic jacet.
To be looked at two centuries from now
By curious eyes. Say, a girl. A boy.
Dragged to the antique cemetery by
Concerned parents to read the worn stones in their
Quaint lettering. Scoured by weathers. Scathed
By sun. Are those *my* bones lying under the headpiece?
Was it a century? Two centuries? Three?
Do they bind up my headstone with hoops of steel
To keep it from crumbling? Is there any bone
Of mine still beneath the stone?
Is there anything? A ring of gold, mayhap,
Which tells of woman? Which tells
Of child beating up the womb
Like horses out of Ischia, as poets say?
Or a tooth or two? A filling by
Dentist, long dead, in whose chair I sat
Moving my tongue in comment on the current scene?
Suffering pain? Feeling the needle go in
To deaden me with novocaine?
Or a knuckle-bone—or kneecap—or two?
Quoths the merry owl with his whoo?
Is there a hemlock, that tree
Of death, as poets construe? For me
The death-tree? Hemlock for me?
Owl hooting in the hemlock-tree?
Give me pause. I ask an entr'acte—a chuckling time.
Break the eons. Stay momentarily
The abandon—abandonment—of sea.

Part it, as once the red water was
For armies of Israelites. Give me
A grimace of jawbone—if jawbone there be.
A dimpling of delicate laughter in the dust.
If dust there be. The dusty leavings of me.
My scraps. Thighbones. Knuckles. Kneecaps.
But the point I want to make is simply this:
I don't want to lie in a grave. My bone
Labeled with a hardy stone—
Cut with lettering of some quaint century.
Among the giggling cheeks of boy and girl.
Laughing, half in fear, nervously.
Impatient of the hemlock and the owl.
Wanting to be off with her jiggling curl.
Pulled by parents. By their haunted eyes.
Thinking they make good case for history.
Thinking they educate the child, showing him
Gravestone, hemlock, owldom.
I see in the ground the new-laid body. The
Body of me. I feel
Time pass. I see
My bones whiten into skeleton.
I feel silly. The whiteness of me! The
Helplessness! The nakedness to any eye
Coming to brave the owl and the hemlock-tree.
I am a public spectacle, at last!
The careful arrangement of my bones
By that mortician I remember well—
His hands upon my utter clamminess.
His owl-eyes peering down at me
Unruffled. With a merry whoo!
Faces passing to and fro
To bid farewell to my slack dust.
Wondering faintly where, mayhap, had gone
That spirit in his nostril, called *ghost.*
That thing which animated his merry skeleton.

Now that three centuries have come and gone—
Or so. More or less. At last.
And I have come, as golden girls all must.
And the jawbone in my skull. If skull there be.
Tongueless in its laughter. And I have come to know
My helpless disarray in dust and molecule. I am
A name upon a stone in a realm of owldom.
A flaccid clown. A petty politician of space and time.
I am not comfortable, but I endure.
Step right up, ladies and gentlemen! It's free.
Read my stone which marks me
Timeless as Caesar or Rameses. Note—know
The worn letters of my late century
Cut in stone, quaintly naming me.
Come. Do not whisper. Breathe easily.
Click your tongue at time. And time's mute way.
Roll your eyes as you approach some day
This dusty spectacle—who know
Nothing of me. Nor of night or day—
Nor of the universal circus—nor even
Of so little a thing as this, under heaven,
The owldom of one man's late surcease—
Who is your wasted stone—your quaint sideshow.

JACK CRAWFORD, JR.

GREEN HIDES: LINES TO A PALE LADY

In the long smoldering slumber of dawn
Stained on a skin drawn to span the world,
Eye coldly in a leathery embryo
Hatchings of plains, an appalachian
Ridge, and a valley where the green belly,
Franked with a surcharge of rivery red,
Forks into a tail, tells what the green hides . . .

I

Under the embers of this nether sphere
Slides an animal on tunneling tide
Tooling its alley, aisle and artery
Miles from the combers' swell, funneling sea
Inland beyond the dunes to ponds, which once found
Are tapped; and in the brackish merge, all veins
Surge for the trapper of the lost ichors.

Solvent in the maze of a slough's veneer,
Among the leads, lies an aorta-wide
Stream (around the size of an ottery)
Which he rings with the loop of a tree
Snare or a snapping weir, staked to leave him drowned
As sprung, on the flood's make; and the tide wanes
To ripples in the piping of far breakers.

Come dawn on the wan tract he slips a fin
Collar-deep in the icy burn, to quake
At the cold spark that connects him to flows
Of ocean in vessels; liquors that fleet
As he fingers along a slippery wall
Feeling for the animal inside, finds
His furry flesh always a caught surprise.

On this sponge with nothing to underpin
But abyss of ooze and a yawning lake,
He treks with his burden slung back through doze
Of rushes and a sedge sweet in the sun's heat,
Buoyant as the tussocky spring and tall
As a man can stand, till the spring unwinds
At the landfall, and he follows its rise.

In the shed he girds the tail, each tendon,
Cuts the fur between them—but you can't skin
Otter like you peel a rat. You've got to slice
Free the fat on the slit between the hide
And body, before you loosen the paws;
Lance its lobes and eyes, then pull off the pelt.
And the meat rank with fish?—He throws it out.

Fell in hand, he shapes the plank he skinned on
To fancy the dank hide, tenses it thin
As he can to the plat's end, tacks it twice
To the wood tight as a vise on each side,
Lets it swing in shadow till time for taws
And tanner's bark, or until it is gilt
With a dawn burnt beyond tanning or doubt.

II
Slowly skin cools in the sidle of stars,
And the dapple scores configure the cure
With contours and colors the skeleton key
To later roughs of a route etched in sand,
Poke-dyed in bark or inked on a tanned hide—
Every chart and charter since drawn by man,
Each one an heir to the skin side of fur.

Not far at all from skinners' scimitars
Dries that tawny, townless savanna moor,
The apogee in a stage of ennui
Mesaless, without lakes, a nomad's land
Crossed only by coulees fast with oxide
Of iron, plain stands for expanses in tan
Which hover our days like a leveller.

From the same plane stems a green ocher chain
Born of a chine streak in the tracker's eye,
A ridgebone bridging kit and caboodle
Beginning to end silvicultures back,
Before the graven mottle became the green
Bottle which infixes a man with mood
Instead of woods ingrained in lacquer fat.

Though the valleys between the fur and pain
Come minted green when the skin's hung to dry,
As they wizen and fall to the scruple
Stone, they turn to barrens, never to smack
Of the limp rank nether vale again, weaned
Except in the womb of a trapper's brood
Who remember an underbelly plat.

Prongs of taper lightning overlie
The papery whole with a gravity
Past our own, grown by animals inside
Till orphaned in severing, the fiery
Branches appear burned, never to menace
Again; but gules gullies are a man's trap,
And one day the deluge's swells recur.

Let a mapper on canvas or papyri
Paint features of a land, morass or sea:
Let all our pens and calipers be tried:
Scan all surveys Mariana to eyrie:
And glean all the green ochers, siennas,
Umbers the earth can muster: No man's map
Can ever touch the skin side of a fur.

You, pale lady, with the fur against your fawn!
You with the thin swan skin more softly pearled
Than sable! You, pale lady, in cameo,
Missed the contours of your chapel nation:
Red rivers, appalachia streaked, valley
Dry, and all that tawny unexplorable spread.
You are the legend—and the maps your hides.

JOHN CREIGHTON

A DOUBLE HAUNTING

Man will be always haunted by his world
—Though he should escape for a time by sealing himself
In plexiglass abstractions, equipped with filtered air
Pumped from underground purifiers, though he should
Call green his enemy, inoculate his heart
Against the virus of mutability,
Quarter the ocean and atmosphere, fouling what's left
With oil-slick and fumes, excreta of his contempt
—Even before the wind changes, the tide returns him his folly
He will ache unexpectedly for the boyishness of plants,
For rogue elephant grasses, the Yarra Bank crankiness
Of trees, jungles to sweat in and out of,
And the head-down happiness of beasts with their innocent loyalties.

And the world, in its turn, for a time will be haunted by man
—Even after his vapour-trails have scrawled their Omega
Over the evening heavens, kindly or gross
His shadow will fall on the ground and the beasts in their browsing
Tremble a moment remembering, the rivers and seas
Will dwindle to rivers and seas, the leaves and the vines
Sigh in the simpler wind for the old touch of Latin
And for men to push through them and set up a camp in the clearing.

BRUCE DAWE

FAN LETTER TO GLENN FORD

Glenn, some things never end.
Human Desire, for instance,
that great movie starring
Good and Evil, two old-timers
brought back each year
by popular demand. That diesel
engineer you played was a man
the boy in me could love.
So cool at the throttle and horn,
ram-rodding freight and sleepers
in and out of Trenton, New Jersey,
that ideal fishing hole out west
in the back of your mind, trouble
in the front. And faced with trouble,
the worst kind of trouble, woman trouble,
you tipped your oil-scarred cap
and barreled out of town,
the muscles in your jaws
working things out for themselves.

Evil, of course, destroys itself,
feeds on itself, and in the end,
is its own worst enemy.
The evil switchman, Broderick Crawford,
drunken wife-beater, and murderer
of the evil rapist, bears this out.
Milton, the poet, would have approved,
perhaps had a hand in the script.
Gloria Grahame is solid as Eve,
brought up to date by cause and effect:
cigarette burns riveting shoulder and breast,
and that weak mouth always begging
for the worst, which never quite happens.
Wife to the drunken switchman,
her wet lisp led you down
from the high chair of engineers
into the cinders that ruin
a good man's vision of the straight track,
the thin V that pins down
the wide-screen horizon
west of Cleveland. Glenn,

I too believe in Evil.
With you, I climbed
that Union Pacific beauty,
opened her throttle wide for Utah
where good people end their lives
cut off from tired drunks
and women who deserve their scars.
How could we know
that twenty cars behind our smiles,
linked to us by steel,
the despondent killer has killed, again,
the only thing he ever loved,
or that we tow his sorrow west
to the end that cannot end?

RICK DEMARINIS

PASSED A SWAN

Passed a swan this afternoon.
Same one I'd seen crinkling
lake water sealed to the belly
of his image.
Passed him lunging for a scrap
in roadside rubble,
an angel
with wings wrenched back,
orange legs spraddled
among burnt stumps
and flattened beer cans.
Passed him in the old car
going north by the palisades,
surprise clamped to my brow
all the way home.
Same as when I saw a dolphin
leave the ocean throwing away
diamonds. Saw his flukes say:
so long! as he sounded.
Keep carrying with me the dancer
who turns in fathoms of blood
or stamps among stones
where no one expects him.

SONYA DORMAN

SQUASHES

Like beheaded geese plucked to their
    yellow skin they lie in the shade
Of an obscene but stalwart little forest
    of thick leaves,
Lost in all that heat, in a world they
    never made.

Brought into the house they lose their
    murdered, meat-shop look—
I place them along the stone wall on the
    porch,
Their necks entwined like abstracts of
    yellow mandolins accompanied by a
    book.

In a manner of speaking I have arranged
    for their rescue—
They are handsome as a Braque,
    accented by that important,
Lyric-looking volume with the jacket of
    dark blue.

Always and always the suspicion mounts
As we accumulate our world around us
    and see it rot
That, given the given, it is what we do
    with a thing that counts.

58

Which is not to say that now or ever one
    will quite be done
With whatever dreams itself to be in us
    at first glance,
Little glutted, yellow-bellied, murdered
    geese lying in the sun.

But if on closer look, the mandolins are
    warted, not quite so sleekly gold,
And the wind shallows through the
    pages of the book,
We shall have made our passions for a
    little while do as they are told.

CHARLES EDWARD EATON

A JUMPER

for Thomas James White Hawk, condemned to the electric chair

> He held the state high
> school pole vault record of
> 13 feet, 7½ inches in 1965.
> —from the *Minneapolis Star*

We shall not let him
float out through the bars
in the odor of pea soup
      but
fit in the cage of his fingers
the warden's golden
curtain rod and
unlock the air of
the concrete yard for the
seconds
to a last vault:

who will ever hear
ever see him
moving in the moccasined dark
toward the law's
wall   that *this time* will
not bend him down who
bursts the inevitable
jolt   steals up
his loins
learns
too late his name?

DAVID ALLAN EVANS

FOR HIMSELF IN THE SPRING

We die. Sometimes suddenly without preparations
or preamble. Our knowledge of night depth-sounds
into the rock below the garden and Persephonic
is the perfume of the flowers. Nobody believes it.
Least of all, the people who never knew us.

We die. Spring sharpens our awareness
of this impossibility as autumn stills
the mystery of our underwater gardens.

Love, the black crows have come out of the white woods
and sit now in the regeneration of our absolutes.

Every eye is dilated with the ache
of the widening sun. Doors shut across the park.
Blinds are drawn in the afternoon bedrooms.

We die. I sing all the months of spring
when I see you. And I have looked for you
in every spring since I stumbled
upon my beginnings preceding all my layers
of beginnings again and other beginnings.
Which makes the song re-troactive.

Sometimes I sit at the window in the dusk
and sing to the joy of the nothing there
but something coming towards your life
that will lay its small exciting hands on mine

And who ever hearing me sing for the child
to perpetuate you, who ever watching me listen
for your step, who ever seeing me look at you,
who, who would ever believe we die?

We die. Already I know some of the dead.
Let us go to the lake then for the day.
I would just like to lie in your arms
and imagine the places where we will go together
after this one

a farm-house in the sky above the Opeongo Trail?

coral-head castle under the lake
close by our meeting-place at Bath?

Love, hold my hand. We die.
Especially in the spring the long-time lovers
sense it

and guard each other

with resurgence

and renewal

JOAN FINNIGAN

MUSIC OF THE SPHERES

I
"music please" and the man at the telescope
looks and listens looks and listens and waits

this vulgar Beethoven is thrust
like a crude vase on the mind's mantelpiece
to interrupt the monotony of space

pastoral valleys in a calculating brain
green waters to catch a falling star

yet it is partly true,
the star falls away incredibly
and what the old German scratched on paper
was true
of the giant nebulae that rolled away
past him into his green and silent night

II
it's only the last centimetre
that makes music

Ptolemy's little golden wheels
will shine for ever, they are laid
and numbered in silk-lined boxes,
in their time
they were the movement of God's brain
smoothly timeless on their jewelled bearings

the spheres are broken and their music
is war
they do not keep time with each other
for time bends

it is vain to cloud the sky over
with coarse noise to cheat the silence
for the silence slips through
a ghost of thin dust

it's only the last centimetre
where there's space enough for music
and for me to walk about in it listening

III

if they do
catch creation in the act
if they do
reach an edge that is really an edge
and not just the edge of their minds
if they do
trace time and space into
a new multifoliate rose

if they do
I'd like to stand at the last centimetre
where the long elipses touch down

and listen
to the old music taking the strain of the new
and putting out notes like snowdrops
as if
there had been no crushing weight of winter

ROBIN FULTON

WORLDLINESS

Worldliness is your enemy.
Never think otherwise.
It does not tolerate for long
love that you love.
From where the pure lament
played on ancient instruments?
To what is a sob a response?
Trumpets lift our spirits up. To where?
The world is entangled with
continued decay and death.
It courts but abhors
the opposite it needs.
Entrapped in its laws
it ravages love,
hacks at truth,
weeping, weeping it must do
what is incumbent upon it to do!

How moving to think
that from time to time
a white horse does come
bringing a beautiful
redeemer in human form.

ARTHUR GREGOR

POEM FOR JOHN BRADLEY

(Burned to death at Smithfield, England, 1410)

John Bradley you give soothing
to nostrils blistered with docility;
flesh indentured into char through choice
had greater dignity to uphold
than man-made manna for a cause to live;
this pasty thick fat of our lives
is suddenly rank and cheap as words
to keep us undiseased in an epidemic world.

What thread of your imagined face
so fine now makes all things I look at
lovely to be near and quick as wood
that took up flame and turned your scream to song.

You said "a Priest's power was as little
as a street sweeper's, and no man could convert
bread into the body of Christ."
        Yet what a taste you give whole wheat
        what a sweet swallowing my hand
        fumbles the tablecloth of your few crumbs.

Your words were burned until
even bones were ashes
random with the wind-seed;
and the watching mob's amusement
snaps even now with hyena jaws
through the massive bones
of a once more savage world.

Quiet fires from woodlands
flicker cadences of autumn night.
Ashes give off cedar and cypress odors

Trees renew.
Leaves burn in front of houses
suburbia smoulders;
quiet figures leaning with rakes
stand in solitude and through the smoke-scrim
stare, hypnotized
the smell of burning on them
without words among them
the last gestures of a wood-passion
from an ancient image on a hill.

S. GRESSER

TRAVELLING

1

Mountains, lakes. I have been here before
And on other mountains, wooded
Or rocky, smelling of thyme.
Lakes from whose beds they pulled
The giant catfish, for food,
Larger, deeper lakes that washed up
Dead carp and mussel shells, pearly or pink.
Forests where, after rain,
Salamanders lay, looped the dark moss with gold.
High up, in a glade,
Bells clanged, the cowherd boy
Was carving a pipe.

And I moved on, to learn
One of the million histories,
One weather, one dialect
Of herbs, one habitat
After migration, displacement,
With greedy lore to pounce
On a place and possess it,
With the mind's weapons, words,
While between land and water
Yellow vultures, mewing,
Looped empty air
Once filled with the hundred names
Of the nameless, or swooped
To the rocks, for carrion.

4686848772

2

Enough now, of grabbing, holding,
The wars fought for peace,
Great loads of equipment lugged
To the borders of bogland, dumped,
So that empty-handed, empty-minded,
A few stragglers could stagger home.

And my baggage—those tags, the stickers
That brag of a Grand Hotel
Requisitioned for troops, then demolished,
Of a tropical island converted
Into a golf course;
The specimens, photographs, notes—
The heavier it grew, the less it was needed,
The longer it strayed, misdirected,
The less it was missed.

3

Mountains. A lake.
One of a famous number.
I see these birds, they dip over wavelets,
Looping, martins or swallows,
Their flight is enough.
The lake is enough,
To be here, forgetful,
In a boat, on water,
The famous dead have been here.
They saw and named what I see,
They went and forgot.

I climb a mountainside, soggy,
Then springy with heather.
The clouds are low,
The shaggy sheep have a name,
Old, less old than the breed
Less old than the rock
And I smell hot thyme
That grows in another country,
Through gaps in the Roman wall
A cold wind carries it here.

4

Through gaps in the mind,
Its fortifications, names:
Name that a Roman gave
To a camp on the moor
Where a sheep's jawbone lies
And buzzards, mewing, loop
Air between woods and water
Long empty of his gods;
Name of the yellow poppy
Drooping, after rain,
Or the flash, golden,
From wings in flight—
Greenfinch or yellowhammer—

Of this mountain, this lake. I move on.

MICHAEL HAMBURGER

FATHER AND CHILD

I. BARN OWL

Daybreak: the household slept.
I rose, blessed by the sun.
A horny fiend, I crept
out with my father's gun.
Let him dream of a child
obedient, angel-mild—

old No-sayer, robbed of power
by sleep. I knew my prize
who swooped home at this hour
with daylight-riddled eyes
to his place on a high beam
in our old stables, to dream

light's useless time away.
I stood, holding my breath,
in urine-scented hay,
master of life and death,
a wisp-haired judge whose law
would punish beak and claw.

My first shot struck. He swayed,
ruined, beating his only
wing, as I watched, afraid
by the fallen gun, a lonely
child who believed death clean
and final, not this obscene

bundle of stuff that dropped,
and dribbled through loose straw
tangling in bowels, and hopped
blindly closer. I saw
those eyes that did not see
mirror my cruelty

while the wrecked thing that could
not bear the light nor hide
hobbled in its own blood.
My father reached my side,
gave me the fallen gun.
'End what you have begun.'

I fired. The blank eyes shone
once into mine, and slept.
I leaned my head upon
my father's arm, and wept,
owl-blind in early sun
for what I had begun.

II. NIGHTFALL
Forty years, lived or dreamed:
what memories pack them home.
Now the season that seemed
incredible is come.
Father and child, we stand
in time's long-promised land.

Since there's no more to taste
ripeness is plainly all.
Father, we pick our last
fruits of the temporal.
Eighty years old, you take
this late walk for my sake.

Who can be what you were?
Link your dry hand in mine,
my stick-thin comforter.
Far distant suburbs shine
with great simplicities.
Birds crowd in flowering trees,

sunset exalts its known
symbols of transience.
Your passionate face is grown
to ancient innocence.
Let us walk for this hour
as if death had no power

or were no more than sleep.
Things truly named can never
vanish from earth. You keep
a child's delight for ever
in birds, flowers, shivery-grass—
I name them as we pass.

'Be your tears wet?' You speak
as if air touched a string
near breaking-point. Your cheek
brushes on mine. Old king,
your marvellous journey's done.
Your night and day are one

as you find with your white stick
the path on which you turn
home with the child once quick
to mischief, grown to learn
what sorrows, in the end,
no words, no tears can mend.

GWEN HARWOOD

SPANISH SOLDIER

1

At the window
the grey soldier stares through his tender face
but the dark air has opened
and he stretches his arms out to feel the weight
of the fever.
Rain sleeks the gutters—
only the *clicklisp* of a passing blonde.
Someplace the king is dying and
the soldier braces his drunken flesh.

And I have come no closer to that savage place
than pink wives or joking husbands.

2

I have ridden golden stallions across the brittle air
plunging swells on their convulsed bodies.

I took my sword from the sparkling witches
but sleep has ripened in me. It is time.

3

I
looked back and
the last sky was caving in, swamping
the church, monks stunned
flat in spirals
I cupped my ears as
space snapped and the gulls
streaked through me.

4

Someplace inside him the king's eyelids are sewn.
Death makes love to the soldier's limp body.

C. DAVID HEYMANN

DEAD DUCK

A rotary motorscythe is an instrument of magic:
It eats the grass like hate.
Hate hits back in dank weather:
A tall wet blade shorts the spark circuit,
A cough, and the snarl's earthed:
The bruised silence sneers—
A two-stroke is a devil to re-start hot.

I curse the long grass after a damp September.
The battered blue chopper snags on molehills;
Each jolt judders the clutch-catch into my thumb;
The starter cord breaks and I scream obscenities at it;
Sweat drops fall on the rusty grass-box as I heave away.

The impeller chops windfalls; children's gew-gaws
I am sick of picking up I deliberately suck in;
Wood quoits, slashed sorbo, thunder into its throat:
I am the Leveller, no mere chore's idiot:
But the pose does not relieve my mow-ricked back.

In the tough water-grass, whoa! A crouched black back of
feathers!
Immobile as the men on Green Beach: sod you, mow
over it.

A hint stir of maggots deflects me:
I fear the sickly corpse smell that makes you puke:
I shrink the blade-slashed elbow bones and bits of slung
guts:
A decapitated frog once pulsated like a red and green
purse trying to run.

The damned machine won't stop: the clutch has gone:
Up and down I'm dragged, flanking the bird.
It lies in a mound of twitch and clover, a pearly dew-
            decked grave:
One white feather trimming the black, the underedges
            seeping.

Among the unmowable edges, its quick short life!
Black furball first like wind on the water only, subwing,
Then after innumerable circlings among the gnats,
Running its own strip of streamside,
A quick beak for territory, the little quick mutters of
            unseen matings:
Who notices the small windfall shadows scuttle back to
            the cress?

I found another in the orchard, more like loam.
What kills them? There were live coots, scuttling for
            safety.
But it was the dead ones that followed me indoors
Long after the vortex was silent. Most die unnoticed.

I probably never saw that coot alive: nor did no one.
Its tail flicked in the sunshine of three seasons,
Then it sank into the grass. The meta-questions
I would not have escaped by mowing up the remains:
Nor do I answer them by leaving them undisturbed—
A small still tussock disfiguring my lawn.

DAVID HOLBROOK

WHIPSNADE

African larynx, coming out of a hawthorn bush:
I hold my baby like a lifebelt.

I could easily throw him to the Kodiak bears.

Two feet from a tiger's puzzled mask, he makes
His love-noise appropriate for Pussy: my nape hair bristles.
Why does the dead-pan Polar bear, like a ridge of snow-rug,
Pendulum his great head into the wind, on those massive
                                                    claw-props?
He is like an ice-berg shaking its grey head:
Silently we retreat with the Arctic metronome in our blood.

What does baby think? I remember Tolstoy
With his head in the bear's mouth, the teeth razoring.
Tom is as puzzled as I am by the enigmatic muzzles,
I can tell that: neither his soft, 'Ah!' nor his angry, 'No!'
Generate a flicker over the Siberian doggedness
Of the tall wood wolf that shrinks into its squint, and schemes.

Does baby take in anything? Will he understand better
Why, in his story book, the Town fled the Happy Lion?
The elephant and the rhinoceros were too big for him—
He simply gazed at their muddy sides as he does at landscape.

Only a llama calf alarmed him of all the animals,
Because as he stroked its breast its neck did a U-turn
And sniffed the top of his head, hard.

Three weeks later, penned behind railback chairs,
A dead-pan polar bear cub rocks on prodigious muscles,
With a hint of razor-sharp menace in his expressionless mouth,
The wolf-scheme in his eyes, and even the puzzled frown of
the tiger.

I remember a television interview,
The 'Jim Conway morning show,' Chicago:
'What kind of a man do you think did this murder?'
The girl's father answering this impertinence:
'Brother—you tell me!'

DAVID HOLBROOK

THE SCHOOL OF NIGHT

What did I study in your School of Night?
When your mouth's first unfathomable yes
Opened your body to be my book I read
My answers there and learned the spell aright,
Yet, though I searched and searched, could never guess
What spirits it raised nor where their questions led.

Those others, familiar tenants of your sleep,
The whisperers, the grave somnambulists
Whose eyes turn in to scrutinize their woe,
The giant who broods above the nightmare steep,
That sleeping girl, shuddering, with clenched fists,
A vampire baby suckling at her toe.

They taught me most. The scholar held his pen
And watched his blood drip thickly on the page
To form a text in unknown characters
Which, as I scanned them changed and changed again:
The lines grew bars, the bars a Delphic cage
And I the captive of his magic verse.

But then I woke and naked in my bed
The words made flesh slept, head upon my breast;
The bed rode down the darkness like a stream;
Stars I had never seen danced overhead.
'A blind man's fingers read love's body best:
Read all of me!' you murmured in your dream.

'Read me, my darling, translate me to your tongue,
That strange Man-language which you know by heart;
Set my words to your music as they fall;
Soon, soon, my love! The night will not be long;
With dawn the images of sleep depart
And its dark wisdom fades beyond recall.'

Here I stand groping about the shores of light
Too dazzled to read that fading palimpsest
Faint as whisper that archaic hand
Recalls some echo from your school of night
And dead sea scrolls that were my heart attest
How once I visited your holy land.

A. D. HOPE

MY SMALL AUNT

died in a dust of lions; her Africa
was secret as her body and arrived
like the biblical robber by night, by darkest night;
that night, however, was the cinema's:
where, there before her, high and bright, and wide
as love, it stretched its radiant sinister light.
And by the foreground clump of pampas grass
shone the pride.

She knew it all before she saw it all.
Lighthearted as a warrior come home
she absolved its horrors: the bald-necked buzzards,
carrion-content; and in the waterhole
the gross great pigs that float their eyes on scum;
the cough, the red snatched meal, the hot-breathed hazard;
in what sense the pride goeth before that fall—
the hunted one.

Was she the hunted or the hunter or both?
At home, the click and tick of cup and clock
chattered like north itself. Hunted by pain
and tireless hunter of the secretive moth,
what chilly key should she turn in a useless lock?
At dawns, the raw boughs rocked by her cold pane.
But in her sun slept lions, chockablock
with blood and sloth.

She queued for her ticket in the stale winter street
and, step for step, the mean wind cried like a ghoul
in her ear and flourished its trash and her blue eye wept.
But closer and close, the aromatic heat
and the flat trees; and like a homing soul
she met the spaces the hot grasses kept
and met the motion of four soundless feet:
the paced prowl.

Hunted and hunter. Too brave to be sad,
the fear of pity fixed her like a stare.
Sharp, starry hunters, luminous Orions
whirled in her sleep. Taking her cup in bed
she drank unsweetened courage black and clear.
In their gold ruffs waited the shining lions,
violent and sunny lords who never had
pity or fear.

JOSEPHINE JACOBSEN

IT STAYS

What fills this house,
slides under
the weather-stripping,
wagging branches
plugged with leaves
or buckled with fruit
will never be married.

If I grow friendly,
regard it calmly
as one strokes a child's
head talking to somebody
else, it leeches
in, breeding
its own disorder.

And if I lie down
under it, make
it as real as what
I have become,
it grows around me,
shoves its way
into my arms.

Jasmine, we shake
the air and vines
catch fire.
Flesh of the inner
flower, eyes
above me coming
through leaves.

The old nibble of lies
in the dark, vines
bursting fragrant
against my hair,
hurting my face.
They climb the walls
like toads, open

their tropical mouths
crowded with roots,
saying, you've got to
feed us, cracking
the paint, the plaster,
shaking me, nothing
I'll ever tame.

SHIRLEY KAUFMAN

BIRD, FOX, AND I

Turn now, my tongue, on such red syllables
As catch the bird that feathers at the box
Eating the seeds. I, too, am hungry. A fox
Is in me chasing its ruffled tail all day.
Bird, fox, and I are in the winter.

Tables

Of crusts, corn, pecked-shells make my cardinal
Whistle. The fox in me will curl as well
With sex as food. But, red tongue in me, say
What nouns of bread, what adjectives of lust
Will sing me like the bird in trees of hope,
Or like my fox bed down my sleep in trust?

I hunger in my shadow for my shape.

Birds fed on winter branches yet will shake
Blue cloudy music overhead in June;
And all the hundred thousand foxes, having slept
Warm with their flesh by January moon,
Will, in the daisy dawns and greens, awake
Cold-nosed, to hunt again.

                                But I am kept
Unpeaceful. Talk of the days spouting their snow,
The wild clocks worrying the mind with reasons,
Weathervanes and vanities come and go
Like firebird and the fox who are but seasons.

Therefore, my tongue, be bolder yet. Summon
For thirst the rooded wine, vermilion, vast,
And drink it down me. And for my famine,
Chew in me hunks of that rough bread, God's taste
Along the bones.

He'll rock my fox to sleep by me in love,
And in me let the bird's red music rave.

ARNOLD KENSETH

SUMMER STUDENT

In the blue-eyed day I see mirrors
Because the girl in the button blouse has eyes
Blue as gray is blue; and soft terrors
Run through me because she is in the hays

And warmth, in the tawn mows heaped and round
With summer. O all the noontimes of the fields
Compare her, and she is seen in the shields
The sun hangs, and on the walks of sound.

Reflections tell of her white rising
To water songs, as if I saw egrets stalking
In the green clear streams; as if, nereid,
She swims my skin, spinning her snow ahead,

Her breath within my breath carousing.
I day-dream her. Doubtless, she will be walking,
Long-stepped and sure, into my winter,
The wind prowling, blowing her summer dress.

ARNOLD KENSETH

DERELICT FREEHOLD

All things are possible inside this house—
   it may be no house but a book, or fantasy
   of a sleeping egg, and we are words or shells.
The impossible is what happens daily in this house.

The chances of this house are millions against,
   odds on nothing—and yet we're here—perhaps.
   The architect a man of gargoyle wit,
nameless and called in curses, dead now, no regret.

The doors hang, roofs pitch, rooms go gangling about
   in the aimless, then stop. All windows jam
   open or shut; the garden wild and flowering,
hedges curved and poplars look like bars at night.

No one knows who comes and goes, or what the news;
   the people ghostly and the ghosts full-fleshed.
   Dust is indestructible. The spirit fades, then sparks
the light-bulbs, flames the house, and will not sleep.

We're all in this together—share the bed
   with corkscrew, rat, and lover; find the bath
   resounding song; the smell of leaves that creep
about the floor, and stairs that talk too much.

What if—what if the walls were glass to enemy
   outside? Why is touching mirrors meeting hands?
   Are the trees watching, do their branches semaphore
attack? Why is the plumbing so rebellious?

There is something must be done; some say
    change the locks, and others, smash the door.
    And rising dustbins barricade the back;
our flag has fallen from the taxman's map.

Suppose in holy lunacy one took an axe
    and dealt with breaking chairs, renaissance beds;
    suppose a flying jug connected with a window,
pump, light, and dryer linked—to making toast?

Suppose surrender to the flash of black
    beat down the walls and hose the rubble out;
    this house is all things possible and new,
naked to the searching fingers of the day.

TIMOTHY KIDD

A GARLAND FOR EMILY

A Sequence of Four Poems in Memory of Emily Dickinson

1. IN THE HOUSE OF EMILY DICKINSON

At this small table, hardly
Bigger than a checkerboard,
She told with birdlike hand
The coming of the word.

Over the square-paned casement
A muslin curtain, bright and still.
A hedge away, the country lane,
The fields, the railroad of the will.

She could see out, but they
Could not see in. The heart's long mile
Was all she trod, her world a room.
It did not cramp her style.

A spirit here was not confined,
But wandered high and far—
From yards of death to leagues of life,
From slowest candle to the quickest star.

2. ELEGY FOR EMILY

Robed in her usual white, withdrawn
In her white casket she was borne
Out of the sunny back door, over the lawn,
Along the ferny bridlepaths of May
To the burial ground on Pleasant Street.

The Irish workmen, her friends and servants,
Conducted her in a funeral like a game,
Some grave children's celebration,
The toecaps of their black boots
Burnished with buttercups.

O she was strange and rare
As a Red Indian brave—dark hair,
Pale face, great eyes, rich mouth.
At her throat, she wore in death
A posy of violets, and one pink cypripedium.

With two heliotropes by her hand
She floated over the pansied grass;
Through the hedge of flowering may
Fled like a flock of linnets,
Leaving behind her a buzz of bees.

The sun shone in her grave sprigged with yew,
Scented with earth and flowering trees.
Dark hair, pale face, great eyes, rich mouth—
Her burial was an ascension, for
It is she who now remains, and we,
Alone, are the departed.

3. AT THE GRAVE OF EMILY DICKINSON

Leaving the florist's on the other side of Pleasant Street
With a posy of corn, thistles, rushes, pink immortelles,
I cross the vulgar road you would not recognize, and turn

Into the burial ground. Behind its black iron railings
Your father's tall stone still casts his shadow over you.
But on your other side, Lavinia—one you loved.

Being apart, in this hilly Amherst graveyard haunted
By weathered flags on worn tombs of forgotten warriors,
Flags whose faded stripes, extinguished stars

The sunset glows through as if they were of glass—
Surrounded by obelisks, yews, maples aflame with fall,
Congregationalist, you lie with them, and lie apart.

92

Below the yew, your father's stone, bolt upright. But yours
And Lavinia's lean back a little, half-fastidiously.
"Called back," says the inscription. (Whither?) "May 15, 1886."

Upon your tomb I pressed two autumn leaves, gathered
                                        from my garden,
But the wind flung them away. Behind your tilted stone
I planted the posy of corn, thistles, rushes, pink immortelles.

I have come all this way across the world to speak to you,
As you so often came to speak to me, but found you
Not quite there: myself, remote and blind, not there at all.

Why am I telling you this? As the tears finally flow for you,
I know you are with me, as always, watching these words I write
To one who was also not altogether of this world.

4. EMILY IN WINTER: AMHERST
Born in December, from the start
You knew a sunstruck winter of the heart.

Gales now blow clouds of snowdust ghosts, that bloom
With rainbows round your black-railed room.

I come once more with flowers and alone
To speak with you behind your stone.

You who can move upon the crusted whitenesses
And leave no track, I press

My handprint on the snow, and feel the heat
Above the buried breastbone where your heart once beat.

JAMES KIRKUP

THE DYING GODDESS

The love goddess, alas, grows frailer.
She still has her devotees
But their hearts are not whole.
They follow young boys
From the corners of their eyes.
They become embarrassed
By their residual myths.
Odd cults crop up, involving midgets,
Partial castration, dismemberment of children.
The goddess wrings her hands; they think it vanity
And it is, partly.

Sometimes, in her precincts
Young men bow curly heads.
She sends them packing
Indulgently, with blown kisses.
There are those who pray endlessly,
Stretched full-length, with their eyes shut,
Imploring her, "Mother!"
She taps her toe at these. A wise goddess
Knows her own children.

94

On occasion, her head raises
Almost expectantly: a man steps forward.
She takes one step forward,
They exchange wistful glances.
He is only passing.
When he comes to the place
Of no destination
He takes glass after glass
As her image wavers.
In her own mirror her image wavers.
She turns her head from the smokeless brazier.

CAROLYN KIZER

THE PRESENCE

Something went crabwise
across the snow this morning.
Something went hard and slow
over our hayfield.
It could have been a raccoon
lugging a knapsack,
it could have been a porcupine
carrying a tennis racket,
it could have been something
supple as a red fox
dragging the squawk and spatter
of a crippled woodcock.
Ten knuckles underground
those bones are seeds now
pure as baby teeth
lined up in the burrow.

I cross on snowshoes
cunningly woven from
the skin and sinews of
something else that went before.

MAXINE KUMIN

ON RECEIVING A DRAWING OF YOUR HAND

Today, opening the envelope—
the tracing of your hand, a line
that seems to hold out luck or hope,
a gesture made to charm or bless
all the way from Boston, less
a gift than fortune teller's sign,
a funny way to touch, I guess,

an omen that's far-reaching. Sleight
of hand's our trade, the casual play
of thumb, so still, that's counterfeit;
the brushstroke lines and mole removed
as if their disappearance proved
some loss had eaten you away.
Magician, forger, I have gloved

your touching note; yet it unfolds.
Hand-drawer, I am drawn by you.
Pocketing what the hand withholds
I summon hexes, chants you'd pick,
pieces of bats and frogs, my trick
to call up verses, call voodoo
and jab a pin; I'd only stick

myself, recalling my last birth
when I was ill, how witchcraft left
me breathless: O dark lady, earth-
bound but often traveling light,
my kind, knowing the earth's weight,
your airmail letters used to lift
me up, losing my hands and feet

awhile. You'd think I rose from bed
by plane, banking above Plum Gut,
climbing until I lost my head.
Outside Boston, what would you do
looking for spring and finding my shoe?
What would you do if you saw my foot
there in your yard, sticking up through

the grass like a tulip? Put up a fence?
Where is your wrist? We're amputees,
almost. I gave you my hand once,
the bitten nails and scars and wart.
Today this print, your counterpart,
becomes you; like a seance, sees
my blind spot working its black art,

a way to reach you. Gypsy dear,
love at my fingertips, I've tried,
am learning braille but raising here
always that sketchy day my mind
conjures without relief, a blind
groping: you standing there beside
the car, waving goodbye, outlined

in shadow, like an old snapshot,
someone I must have known somewhere.
The mind clings to such pictures, caught,
Houdini saying *I'll come back!*
Keep the porch light on! For its sake,
although it overturns a chair,
it will not let its mirrors break

and palms the pieces. When we write
of course we say we'll meet again.
I save your letters. But tonight
your hand lies distant as the stars.
And yet some trace remains, endures.
I cannot read the life line, Anne,
only this empty hand on yours.

PHILIP LEGLER

ADAM NAMES THE CREATURES

And him, and him, and then
That big one there in baggy skin,
The stamper. He roars, and sends
Three messages into the air:
Two silver slivers and a wave of dark
—See how it lifts, and bends!

I've seen that darkness since,
Coiled round a tree. It shines,
It rears on air, it rides
(The bending grass divides).
Its tongue goes in and out
Testing the temperature. It twists.

How can I come by all these names?
Never by trying.
The world's too empty, I must make them up.
Is naming lying?
Don't ask me why I do it: I was told.
"Look," he said, "lion, tiger, dog,
Goat," he said, "spider, hog——"
But those don't count, he said them.
A name is what you find.
Outside ? or in your mind?

(When Eve lies down
Her breasts are flat,
Her belly is a bowl.
She has no breasts, but petals,
Bruises of red, that's all.
She has geraniums.)
That's it, that's it,
Geraniums.

Who bit those leaves
Who scooped Eve's silhouette, with one clear stroke?
It has three breasts, it is
An in and out of yellow green,
It is a perfect curve, a woman leaf,
It is an oak.

I know them now.
The world has come to life.
I name you: elephant.
You needn't pull your skin up, now,
Or dress in shadows:
                    I can see you now.

The darkness that the elephant let fall,
Twisting among the grass, I see that too.
Slanting across a tree its colours break.
Striped tree, dividing grass, I see it all.
I understand the world now:
                              Eve; and God;
And snake. I call you snake.

LAURENCE LERNER

THE BURGLAR

*If entrance is effected by a trick—as when
thieves say they have come to read the meter
for example—it is constructive breaking.*
—An article on Burglars by Thomas Power
in *The Observer*, 10th March 1968.

"Gas Company," I said. "I've come to
    read your meter."
The woman in the dressing-gown drew
    back, smiled, turned
and motioned me in. "It's under the
    stairs," she said.
"I know," I said. "I've done it here
    before."

When she brought me a cup of tea I
    took her arm
and with my usual deftness twisted it
    back,
my spare hand clamping a chloroform
    pad
that I always carry with me for
    emergencies
over her lips. Then like
the good judge of women I am I bound
    her over
to keep the peace with sticking tape
    over her chops
and placed her with aplomb upon the
    sofa.

Left to myself,
among a debris of keepsakes, mirrors,
    appliances,
I found nothing I needed: her supply of
    hope
was down to the last tablet.
I ran my fingers through her dresses,
    ransacked
trunks full of dirty linen, even the
    ice-box.
It seems some people live on very little
between times.
Then under the welcome mat some sort
    of key
opened a curious casket under the bed:
it was full of promissory notes and IOUs
and proceedings for a divorce. This was
    not at all
what I imagined when I entered. The
    house had looked rich.

When the dumb blonde came to I was
    busy cramming
her last silk illusions into my bag. I
    apologized
for the mess, but at least it was a chance
for spring cleaning, wasn't it?
And how else do we survive except by
    constructive breaking?

CHRISTOPHER LEVENSON

GOLDEN AGE: MONART, CO. WEXFORD

There was a land of milk and honey.
Year by year the rectory garden grew
Like a prize bloom my height of summer.
Time was still as the lily ponds. I foreknew
No chance or change to stop me running
Barefoot for ever on the clover's dew.

Buttermilk brimmed in the cool earthen
Crocks. All day the french-horn phrase of doves
Dripped on my ear, a dulcet burden.
Gooseberry bushes, raspberry canes, like slaves
Presented myriad fruit to my mouth.
In a bliss of pure accepting the child moves.

Hand-to-mouth life at the top of the morning!
Shabby, queer-shaped house—look how your plain
Facts are remembered in gold engraving!
I have watched the dead—my simple-minded kin,
Once bound to a cramped enclave—returning
As myths of an arcadian demesne.

Hens, beehives, dogs, an ass, the cobbled
Yard live on, brushed with a sunshine glaze.
Thanks to my gaunt, eccentric uncle,
His talkative sister, and the aunt who was
My second mother, from all time's perishable
Goods I was given these few to keep always.

C. Day Lewis

JUDAS SPEAKS

Someone had to take a cool look at him.
Would-be martyr and messianic publicist,
He's everything to make you love him,
And everything to make you distrust him.
He stumps the country, lecturing to misfits,
Undeniably curing hysterics, staging theatrical
Performances of his message, leading starry-eyed followers
Into a nebulous mysticism, and they're believing,
Everyone's dropping into the delusion
That far-out truths are being revealed.
I love him, but someone's got to stop him,
Someone's got to take a cool look.
He doesn't want to compete, he spurns
'I'he profit motive, despises what he calls
The rat-race, says we're being dehumanized
By an alienated society. He's disappointed
With politics and politicians, social rules,
Distrusts all authority and accuses the priests
Of being rotted by dogma and state allegiance.
Well, maybe they are, but someone,
Something's got to hold things together.
You can't turn all values upside down at once.
He adores spontaneity and improvisation,
But he finds work tedious, lives
Parasitically off the crumbs of the
Affluent Society. He wants a world
Where everyone's happy and loving.
He styles himself the Son of God
And proclaims the reign of Love Alone.
These new-style revolutionaries offer
No formulated theory or blueprint

For the future. He merely urges you
To live for the day and swallow prayer
As the ultimate panacea. He's excessively permissive,
And insofar as he has any political aims
These are, quite simply, to opt out of
'The world,' meant pejoratively. His idea
Of redemption for the world is to
Change consciousness through love and such,
And thus change everything. New heaven, new earth!

So far his followers are still a minority
Among the quiet conforming majority
Who are creating the Affluent Society,
But he does twitch a contemporary nerve:
His philosophy may be full of holes
But his followers aren't philosophers
And he doesn't know what he's stirring up.
Their bizarre dress and behaviour are
Gaining currency and his sayings are
Slipping into the prevailing trendy jargon.
His followers don't work: they're apathetic,
Non-productive and irresponsible.
They stand for anarchy, nihilism and self-indulgence.
They are good-hearted but wrong-headed.
His version of Utopia's naive and foolish
But that doesn't disillusion the layabouts:
They lap it up, of course, like the stuff
He serves up at his love-feasts.
His effects are always unpredictable,
And the health-hazard is patent.
He can produce disastrous panics,
Toppling the neurotic over the edge into madness,
Rendering the unwary so helplessly confused
That they physically do harm to themselves.
Deaths occur.

That being said, it would be unwise
To underestimate his long-term effects
On social security, crime and the development
Of the Welfare State. The toleration
Of the Love Revolution would be a disaster
For the whole of society. I've a responsibility
To my family, to my loved ones.
I don't deny he fooled me for a while
And in a way it's my duty to atone.
Of course, some people will call this betrayal.
But let them. I can't help that.

HERBERT LOMAS

AT MIDNIGHT

Who, if I cried, would listen?
Not the high star, nor the ant
    In his armour.

Each moves on a track, obeys
Voices other than mine. Why
    Should they heed me?

The sea, the wind, and the rocks
Do not hear. The grass has words,
    But no answers.

Lord, send me the least of Your
Angels. I have questions
    To ask of him.

Death comes. Hear me, o cruel
Seraph! I desire the pain
    Of your presence,

And the rational fear,
The thinking terror. I must
    Learn what I am.

EDWARD LUCIE-SMITH

TAM RATING

Nothing that always was is really good enough. Not even the sun.
Certainly not the dead rocked in their coffins, nor the lark
suffocated in the light of a million years advancing;
the peace of a watching sky is a babel of dancing
motes, and there is nothing immutable in anyone.

It is no longer sufficient to walk on the same plane as a flower.
There is nothing beneficial in a long sit on a low bench in a park
when a sweep whistle and high through ninety degrees over the
    grass
turns the tulip around and the poplar into an upturned glass.
We must count down the seasons, inverting the hours.

But they have forgotten the exchange. We have given up what
    we had
and, standing as optimistic as a dog, continue to wait
for the thief. But he will not come again. And it is too late
to run after him for the lyrical bone. Good, bad

or indifferent we must take whatever programme has been
    scheduled.
We are a carefully upturned people. One day when the short
cut to an easing of tension has been bottled, we will run to put
away even tears with the open fire, the useless horse and the
    rhyming fool.

There will of course be the few long-skirted bearded unforwardists
but they will soon get around to elimination in the dark
with the dogmatic lover, the involuntary singer and the saint.
And the place where the poem was will be hidden by washable
    paint
by the time the computer has finished with the lists.

ROY MACGREGOR-HASTIE

POSTCARD FROM A LONG WAY OFF

We have arrived,
fallen out from forests, by an unknown route.
The past has been a nightmare of blizzards and
lice in the folds of the flesh. We have come through
virgin lands, hidden deep in drifts, and finally
crept past the ice-locked outposts of a bad age.

For the present
we are secure, holed up in this ancient house.
The walls are waterfalls, the rats ignore us
having long forgotten humans and how to fear.
Huddled we sit, staring to recall that crawl
past warning sheets like crows hung dead from trees.

The window is
a joke. I can blot it out with my hand. And
was that a bird falling? Did its wing rip and
the gale turn on it, howling like a Chinese
legend knifing through the blood? And why, out here,
do wind and world thrash out a frantic ice age war?

Tomorrow? We
journey on. We are supplied with hunger and
memories which still rub sore. Yet something makes
us move, some force which clamps down tight the black ice
wilderness takes whips and drives us on towards
the spaces where only the white noise hurtles.

WES MAGEE

MY COW

The stones rattle on the hillside
in the fog: the brindle cow is lost,
or drunk again on jimson weed.
She wants to fly, thinks
she is flying, but her hooves
run out of air deep in the heart.
She shakes her head like a dog,
and lows with long, dizzy notes
slipping from her throat, the white
depths groaning under the press of flowers.
She is dreaming, and clambering
toward the moon, or a sunrise
spliced into the night.
The light from her bones blinds her,
the soft edges of stones reach out
like bramble fingers, pluck at her ribs,
pinch her ears. She's speaking Chinese
now: "Wan wu chih mu" she bugles,
calling on The Mother to tame
the stones, melt the snow
that burns in her four bellies, get
her back to earth.

I follow two miles in the fog,
find her the lee side of a watertank
in soft repose, belching,
smiling like an old man.

HOWARD McCORD

EFFORT AT SPEECH

Climbing the stairway gray with urban midnight,
Cheerful, venial, ruminating pleasure,
Darkness takes me, an arm around my throat and
      Give me your wallet.

Fearing cowardice more than other terrors,
Angry, I wrestle with my unseen partner,
Caught in a ritual not of our own making,
      panting like spaniels.

Bold with adrenaline, mindless, shaking,
God damn it, no! I rasp at him behind me,
Wrenching the leather wallet from his grasp. It
      breaks like a wishbone

So that, departing (routed by my shouting,
Not by my strength or inadvertent courage),
Half of the papers lending me a name are
      gone with him nameless.

Only now turning, I see a tall boy running,
Fifteen, sixteen, dressed thinly for the weather.
Reaching the street light, he turns a brown face briefly
      phrased like a question.

I, like a questioner, watch him turn the corner
Taking the answer with him, or his half of it.
Loneliness, not a sensible emotion,
      breathes hard on the stairway.

Walking homeward, I fraternize with shadows,
Zigzagging with them where they flee the street lights,
Asking for trouble, asking for the message
           trouble had sent me.

All fall down has been scribbled on the street in
Garbage and excrement—so much for the vision
Others taunt me with, my untimely humor,
           so much for cheerfulness.

Next time don't wrangle, give the boy the money,
Call across chasms what the world you know is.
Luckless and lied to, how can a child master
           human decorum?

Next time a switch-blade, somewhere he is thinking,
I should have killed him and took the lousy wallet.
Reading my cards, he feels a surge of anger
           blind as my shame.

Error like Babel mutters in the places,
Cities apart, where now we word our failures.
Hatred and guilt have left us without language
           who might have held discourse.

WILLIAM MEREDITH

WAKING DREAM ABOUT A LOST CHILD

Misty and cool. Morning. Who are you, with one hand
Combing damp, fair hair, leaning on the other in your bed?
Outside is the Pacific where the sun went last night
And already another one is coming on behind you.
The latch of the cottage chuckles in the wind. You laugh.
The others are sleeping. The prettiness is fading.
You think of your parents—a one-dollar bill and a five-dollar bill.
You see them waking up under the red tile roof
Where your little sisters stay. The one-dollar bill weeps;
The five-dollar bill crumples itself in its hand.
Disinheriting them, you put on your orange-and-yellow dress.

(Here in the East, I stir in sandy bewilderment.
What debilitating rage can I share with this child?
I cannot imagine seventeen. I can barely imagine
The uses of my middle age. I am fit only for waking.)

Now you think maybe the ocean will know the answer.
You don't think on, as I would, *because it keeps vast,
Sliding appointments* or, *because it tidies up the world's wrack.*
You are simply drawn down the beach like bright new wrack.
Leaving the door to creak on the other runaway children,
You moon down to the water's edge in orange and yellow.
You are like a fresh joint tossed into damp sand.

"More promising than I, why are you extinguishing yourself?"
I call out from the dunes of waking,
"Do you know what you're doing?"
And more than your clear, thin "Oh, yes,"
It is your smile that cleaves and ages me.
Is this what it means to be of two generations?
You put a heron's foot into the dawn-strange water.
Who can help what he dreams?
Mist is everywhere. It is damp in this bedroom.

WILLIAM MEREDITH

IN DEFENSE OF THE MAKERS

Forgive the poet of the woods whose prize
Was solitude with birds that first seemed glad,
Yet sang indifferently. He wrung their necks
In verse; but then their silence drove him mad.

Forgive the city poet. His award—
He ended as the shadow of his name;
On the reverse side of rejection they found scrawled
This epitaph: "That's all there is to fame."

Forgive the wandering poet, based nowhere,
Honored with ticket stubs; at the last station
The Dark Lady put him on his train,
With a broken pen and a bottle of salvation.

The poet of the proud cold tower forgive;
Wore his contempt for crown, spat on base glory,
Climbed up to his work intact and whole,
But, falling down, broke on the common story.

Forgive them this: they only wanted words
To live forever, nothing more. For us,
In woods, cities, or anywhere between,
Obituaries are anonymous.

And one look from the tower plainly shows
The whole thing belongs to death whose style is prose.

LEONARD NATHAN

THE DREAM

We are infested with light.
It gathers on the floor of the sea
that tides in the cave of our pelvis;
it sprouts on the limbs of our lungs,
branches over cliffs in our brain,
a bush burning law in a nation.

An organism from an alien world
rocketed down to test and possess
the planet, it feeds on the darkness
that breeds in the core of our cells,
on the unfiltered air in our lungs.
Overnight millions of filaments

root and are thriving. By morning
our skin is transparent, our bones
are black, and we're radioactive,
barbarously bright. Ablaze
with amazement, we stay in our
bed all day, eclipsing the sun

in its orbit. Afraid we'll diffuse,
we don't move, not a muscle
or bone or an eye-beam. Still
by noon we can feel citizens
disintegrating on streets,
murdered by light. Seasons

accelerate. In the wink of an eye
blossoms are apples that ripen
flames, clusters of grapes are coals.
Antlers of deer are torches, and
buffalos burn to a crisp on the spit
of their bones. The sea pulls

to a dead stop. Whales rise like zeppelins.
By midnight the earth is pure mineral
ore, melting to white at its center.
Ravenous, we embark

A. POULIN, JR.

THE HERO ON HIS WAY HOME

A gathering of whiteness before morning
Rough sheets tightened against the wind
Always it is the same kind of beginning
Gifts and wishes   ceremonies of farewell
Slowly the ship leans toward another island
where they will not know your face
though long ago you stopped growing old

Tonight while Orion floats above the mast
and all directions for once seem clear
you dream of losing hold
reckless between the fingers of a god
whose name you can never remember
And you think if only I could begin correctly
I might discover which way to turn

Everything must be lost
wealth   arms   all companions
Your ship groans beneath you
Gray water rattles into the wood
Speak to the dead and what do they say
I died for you please bury me
What can I say to help tell me what can I say

You will remember
the stuck whine of their tongues   years later
in the scrubbed hall
under the sane roof
while your son grows restless by the fire
your wife more cautious and removed

You will feel a hand tremble upon a knee
as if something had always been wrong
and turning you will whisper
to whatever goddess favors that hour
Lady, listen

Gently then she tells you
where it was you were never going

LAWRENCE RAAB

WALKING ALONE

Where the wild poem is a substitute
For the woman one loves or ought to love,
One wild rhapsody a fake for another.
—Wallace Stevens

It is night. For hours I have been walking,
wanting to see you, hoping you might
appear suddenly by the side of the road,
on a bridge, or in the arc of headlights
bending toward me. I have continued

beyond any place you might conceivably be.
Sunk into a dark hollow, between trees
and stone, the river goes where it has to go.
In the cold air I construct long conversations:
whatever we wouldn't say if you were here.

I recite poems. I return home and write more.
You are, of course, attending within them,
beautiful and calm, near a window
or by a bridge before winter. I fix you
safely, where we might find each other.

But something comes between us, like glass
or water, a distance I cannot avoid.
We meet by accident and fall away.
I come back here, compose another poem,
and walk about at night reciting it to you.

Everything I conceive as possible returns
to an ordered page. I wish I were blind.
I wish my fingers would drop off.
What are they doing, writing all this again?

LAWRENCE RAAB

SPRING

Here it is again, here is the one season
Impossible to describe in its tender lechery,
Its melancholy and fierce enjoyment,
Without yielding to the marshmallow softness of almond blossom,
Catching one's heart on flowered thorn.
Once more trees repeat their names: elder,
Pear and lime. A bevy of grass blades,
More anonymous than the stars, pushes itself forward
In a dizzy whirl which sets earth spinning faster.
It is easy to see why Renoir kept on painting the same girls,
Cézanne the same apples,
Degas the same dancers,
Why one hundred and fifty-four sonnets deal solely with love.
One could spend a lifetime on spring alone—
That pink devil with brandished trident,
Disorderly, riotous spring,
Lusty, uproarious season,
When the wind snips clouds into shreds,
Hurls them happily to the ground,
Twangs the bushes, strums on the grass,
Snarls at last year's tattered leaves
And sits down panting, with its tongue out.
Wait now, wait and watch for the rapid passage
Of the tutu-dressed, tiptoe Japanese cherry
Agog with flower under a disapproving sky,
For the little red bracts on the elm (O, all ye elm trees,
Bless the Lord), and the narrowing green landscape.
As lolloping, trollopy spring sprawls over the lawn
Chaffinches stutter into song, the wren goes to't,
Blackbirds whistle, 'Who's your lady-friend?',

And the dark-footed pettychaps flicks, chiff-chaff, through the firs.
Rowdy, bawdy, gaudy spring spills rain and splashes colour;
Wet branches flash like knife blades turned to the sun;
Spongy clouds wipe up the surplus moisture
And the squandered light soaks away into shallow pools,
Three sips to a sparrow. Pigeons stoop in reverse,
White-collar loafers, falling up into the sky.
Every tree is a maypole
With bright ribbons of sound pulled out taut,
And all light long they dance (every tree a May in April)
Until day closes up like a tulip and they flutter into silence.

DENISE SALFELD

FAMILY TIES

Ah, they are martyrs to love.
See how it brims, how much the small house holds.
Sifting the pallid air, it settles like dust
On children, pets and flowers. A sweet infection
Drenches the double bed. Faces are drawn with the care
And strain. Love darkens the windows,
Lurks in the unwashed crocks and the pile of mending.
The family tremble like flies in a simmering web.

They lean to each other. As her words drift by,
Through the miasma small white faces peer.
The guarded children, gathered on the rug,
Play delicately together,
While stifling in its bonds, the baby whimpers.
Love guides the anxious glance, the probing finger,
The corrosive symptom which stabs him like angina
Or warms her to a comfortable ache;
Stirs in the patience of herbs, the sharp injection.
They carry it, bandaged and dosed,
In the car to the family cottage. How can they tame
This dangerous, gay sun which leaps at their eyes?

Lock, lock it out. Together, secure,
They clutch each other and founder,
The soft tongues licking, abased, the changing wounds.
Night swarms the bedrooms, restless, tropical.
Lapped in damp sheets the children twitch and sob,
While the defeated voices softly rising
Maroon them in the cruel tides of love.

PETER SCUPHAM

THE CROSSING

The journey is always return.
What I cannot leave behind I take
with me: my hands like dry vines
torn from a wall, the memory
of strangers, the smell of wet sidewalks
worn into the soles of my shoes.

Just after dawn the river exposes
its wound and I cross a bridge
in love with its own reflection.
A few lights are still on in houses
down river. A rowboat half sunk
in the mud is calling for help.
Even from this distance I can tell
the trees are crippled with age.

I am full of other places and tired
like birds who return in the spring.
I stumble through jonquils the color
of flesh, past holy places
where lovers and children have made
nests in the matted grass.

They are flying flags in the city
of flags, so many at half mast,
so many in my honor. They keep up
appearances. I enter the city
through a gate as old as smoke
and have returned to my own people.

Those beside whom this river
passes always, will they forgive me
the distance? Those without eyes
who count days by fingering notches
on sticks, those who grow thin
in silence, who do not permit
their clothes to touch their bodies,
who have only their names to guide them.

I walk among them. They bow
two by two, with their arms
around one another. The signs
say "Keep Moving," the flowers are stone
faces covered with moss. I had
no idea the dead lived so well.

RICHARD SHELTON

THE ALBURG AUCTION, VERMONT

Turn once   slowly
in this room of blunted knuckles
turn again   beyond the people:
mother's rocking chair rocks us to our seat,
bedposts are free limbs swinging in the air,
a tricycle's round face
has hair and mouth
that we might fondle kiss
take to bed to make a race of newer men.

The voice skips and hops
in the sour body of someone else's bed;
arms pump the air
compressing affection into a finger's wag.
A mouth filled with pennies gushes forth
its love.

As on the naked organs of our lives
skin exposed to be chewed and stung
these things are salve   are
hands laid on our chest
are the people who owned them.

A young husband from the Bronx
hoists a desk to his shoulder;
a hutch staggers down the aisle;
seven clocks are measured for their pulse:
the bidding goes well.
All men will have lovers.

As objects, once begun, release our love—
begin again as people, not as things.
Rungs of chair
a man's crossed arms waiting for supper.

Chair   touched   has presence.
Withdraw the fingers
and there is neither past nor future in this slab of wood.
The man who used it cannot
now be used by me.

Nor in the ragged turning of our lives
may we find a mouth in someone else's bed.
Drag out the husbands and their wives,
smash lamp glass and chamber pot,
burn all things that masquerade as men—
burning, last, our myths
a bonfire in the mind
          raging
seen for miles.

GLEN SIEBRASSE

THE UNGUARDED ROOMS

Madras

Facing the bougainvillea flare in the sun, the abstract
Of palm spikes, landlord's round concrete porch, fire-gutted
        sunset—
Facing the new
Housing Estates exposed to water—
The sea the huts—facing these,

If you leave one of the rooms alone and the windows open,
Whether or not food is there, birds will come in.

We chased out through the balcony adjoining the bedroom
        yesterday,
Though they were as eager to flee as we were to get rid
        of them, two frightened twittering
Sparrows, mild as milk,
Or the deer of old forest India.

Today two husky black and white mockingbird-seeming
Mynahs, were at the window of the sitting room
Trying to come in, when we opened the door.

Noisy intruders, adopting the ways
Of the new rich of this formerly
Traditional place of quieter
Sparrow-still intrigue—
And only a crumb to peck.

If you leave
Rooms of the mind alone, things enter that are even
    less clearly perceived
Than birds are, on the periphery of vision; specters, on
      the rim of reason; outcastes, on the edge
      of the world,
Shadows of shadows, ghosts of ghosts. Remember to close
    the windows

On that part of the mind not occupied.
And keep busy in the other rooms, move about, ceaseless
    as the ceiling fan.
For, starting with sparrows,
Gentle and jungly as deer, you may finally get
Mynah birds—
Excellent mimics, mimes in the mind—the thieves of speech—
Who say, repeatedly, repeatedly, what they do not know.
Repeatedly beyond reason,
In the mind's weak rooms.

HELEN SINGER

BIRTHDAY IN SABULA

Came I in flame July a braling birth
I matched the dripping doctor slap for slap
So came I incandescent: Of myself;
Mother passive, a vessel for my flap
Into the swelter. Cherubs, gnats aflit
About my head: So I imagined it
In my mad fever; now a five-year-old
(Him very own Birthday Boyee, she told
The passing fishermen); I in my fit
Of fatfaced birthday glut. As I cast out
My line the ripples led my eyes about
To her, as she always was: blue, remote;
Not involved with me: Her head high; afloat
In sky; and I, alone, wrapt in the earth.

    Came evil a headless crow, spread wings raised,
a serpent cawing from its neck, agape
within the featherlines, the serpent shape
squoiled lustily. Lost in the moil I gazed
locked in the trance of coiling shapes, the dumb
immersion in the snapping flame, the swirl
of mudgrilled rivers. Came evil my dream
all abroil, black with trilled and fluted furls.
I felt my burning tongue clap hot and full
up, up it grew aburn and filled my skull
levered my eyes apop into the night.

Started in that pull of wings and black, bright
coils I opened out all eyes and stuffed head
cradling my fear, a hot worm in the bed.
Black runners flags came swirling beating wings
brushed past my eyes. Caught up unresisting
in the winged thunderheads that flecked my eyes
I cried round the clot of my rebel tongue
I AM I AM I AM   flashed back, the cove
of quietude in all this flap. Above,
the coiling wings were gone. I drifted long,
cool, a marble vase turned in the lathe of dreams.
The face of ordered thoughts and unmoiled streams
hung near the bed, his voice assured and strong.

Tom Smith

THE COCKS

When the soft owls finish their conversation
And the raucous earthly birds of day take over
Then it is time for the cocks to crow out of memory.

A thousand hills away, and I nine lives from them
Those tribes are silent now to the last generation.
The hills infer the spring, and mustard grows
And the zig-zag grass, and walnuts green their leaves.
But some dark thing has swallowed all the roosters.

And left us here without that morning song
Bounding from roost to roost—*wake up, wake up,*
It's day, it's day, another day has come.
A halloo sounded up and down the valley,
Over the hills and clear away to the sea.
Then, then was the time we had a use for morning
With a strut of feathers rousting out the sun.

Somehow, sometime the small flocks disappeared.
And the coyotes yap out there in the yellow dark
And the crows and linnets ring the harps of morning.

ANN STANFORD

THE DESCENT

*Let us, therefore, bend all our force and thoughts of soul to
this most holy light, that showeth us the way which leadeth to
heaven; and after it, putting off the affections we were clad
withal at our coming down, let us climb up the stairs which at
the lowermost step have the shadow of sensual beauty, to the
high mansion-place where the heavenly, amiable, and right
beauty dwelleth . . .*

—Baldassare Castiglione

As I descend from ideal to actual touch
As I trade all the golden angel crowns
And rings of light for gross engrossing sense,
As I descend Plotinus' stairs
Angel, man, beast, but not yet plant and stone,
The sense of that height clings, the earthen hand

Transmutes again to light, is blessed from black
Through alchemy to rise rich red, green, blue,
Fractions of vision broke from ample crowns.

As I from the mind's distance fall on voyages
I test the strength of water where I walk
And lose the air for wings. I am lifted
As I descend past clouds and gusts of air
As I go down with wind to tops of trees
As I walk down from mountain tops and cold.

As I descend to gardens warm with leaves
As I enter the new morning harsh in sun
I count the earth with all its destinies
Come down to prove what idea does not know.

I descended out of nothing into green
I descended out of spaces where the spare
Stepping stones of islands roughed my way.
I descended into solidness, to dense
And mingled shrubberies where the birds
Alone choose wings for crossing my old sky.

Caught in this day within a sound of hours
Walled into shadows, stripped of multitudes,
I try this spring the climbing up to light.

ANN STANFORD

THE ORGANIZATION OF SPACE

1
Vacancy goes with me as does a sea,
Perfect, round, in all directions sending
All the not-where, where that one is not bending.

Or the wide disk of grain, shadeless of trees,
Empty, and the arch empty, of seeing,
Above, below, unconscious of that being

And the great desert parched of all—
No rock, no shadow—without green or air—
Only salt and dry, that center being not there.

2
Add to the dull disk of sea colors of coral,
A speck of land within bright shafts of water—
Then we have distance and before and after.

Set in the midst of grain a single tree,
And like a magnet pulling into place,
It draws a path across the unlined space.

And in the desert the uprising stone
Cuts into space and makes the skies convene.
Landmarks arise, and in the shade a green.

3
I praise a local vista, clipped or rough.
It makes its variants with sun and frost—
Hill, row, and field—till vacantness is lost.

And from such centering, the wires that join
The farm and town, the seen and unseen line
Can mark out waves' or gravity's design.

Arched like a row of tents with canvas seams,
The sky is propped by pole and guy to show
They hold the circles fixed through which I go.

4
And yet a vacancy, an almost none,
An arching of the mind into a sky
Under which empty fields and barrens lie,

A round of almost gone, a black and sere,
Returns across the vivid local tiers
And turns them to a round, unshaded sea.

Spirit or being, corn-god or harvester,
That sets us deep within the year's concern,
Hold the circumference in which we turn.

ANN STANFORD

FAREWELL TO FARGO: SELLING THE HOUSE

Olivia is dying. Bring your best black dress.
There will be nothing to take back.
The red squirrels gnawed into all the trunks
and devoured everything in the attic.

The summons was rescinded. She still lives.
I have been called to a different funeral:

An ebony elephant. A china invalid's cup,
blue and white, fragile as the tremor of veins
warping an old hand. The dining-room table
that curves into clawed brass feet.

Little heaps of leftovers under plastic,
they stand isolated—
punctuation marks without our sentence.

The purchasers walk among them
choosing what they will reincarnate.
I cannot bear the helplessness
of the objects dying from our lives.

Aimless as a mourner dismissed from the grave,
I wander out to the garage.

I climb the stairs to the loft.
There is a raw sound of scampering
in the dust before my footfalls.

I find Ferd's silver-capped cane
behind the lawnmower.
He died when I was in the second grade—
a fat man in a gilt frame.

Six daughters and two sons, divisible
into workers, the greedy, and dreamers.

Ferd and Peter kept the store.
Olivia kept the books.
Elizabeth kept the house.

Anne painted roses on china
and grapes on canvas.
Claire in a purple velvet gown
played a gold harp.

Julia and Amelia moved, after
the quarrel, across town
and were asked only to funerals.

They've all gone to the wall—photographs:
leg-of-mutton sleeves
leaning on the porch rail,
watch chains linked like beaded portieres.

There were rides on Sunday after Mass,
parasols behind horses.
Sun honed light above the wheat.

The prairie dust silted into every ruffle.
Then they trotted back to town,
to the house harrowed between the trees,
to dinner on the mahogany table,

eating out of the shine of their faces
while the Red River, a block away,
gnawed its banks, roiling northward.

And what did they ride out to see? There is no
tree, no shrub, no rise of land on the plain.

One by one, they died upstairs,
under the great arm of the elm,
and were taken down in narrow chests,
bumping the turn of the bannister,

to be laid among their bean-row dead
beside the road that runs beyond
the eye—a line drawn on empty paper.

Now only one remains, her mind
sieved by the years to pablum, waiting
to be a name laid into the grass.
She does not know the house is sold.

I take the cane back to the house and
lay it on the dining-room table to be bought.

The purchasers are gone.
There is a storm coming.
I stand on the front step.

The elms hover over the emptied house.
Seeds snow down against
the dark sky, platelets spiralling
in a quickening breeze.

Red squirrels on the roof quarrel
in the fevering silence. Chain lightning
shocks heaven into a jigsaw.

The screen door behind me screams
its spring and slams.

KAREN SWENSON

140

I LOOK AT MY HAND

I look at my hand and see
it is also his and hers;
the pads of the fingers his,
the wrists and knuckles hers.
In the mirror my pugnacious eye
and ear of an elf, his;
my tamer mouth and slant
cheekbones hers.
His impulses my senses swarm,
her hesitations they gather.
Father and Mother
who dropped me,
an acorn in the wood,
repository of your shapes
and inner streams and circles,

you who lengthen toward heaven,
forgive me
that I do not throw
the replacing green
trunk when you are ash.
When you are ash, no
features shall there be,
tangled of you,
interlacing hands and faces
through me
who hide, still hard,
far down under your shades—
and break my root, and prune my buds,
that what can make no replica
may spring from me.

MAY SWENSON

TONIGHT

On this night of low mist
the ghosts of all the babies
rise through the earth crust

From eggshell bones
from bones like powdered sugar
the milky ghosts escape
the ancient dust

Nameless, born of the nameless
dawn tribes, they were scattered
by forest path, left in the sooty cave

Some were the fated first born
hurled into that fiery god-mouth
while the far first cities wailed

Tiny girl-wraiths, fern-like, uncurl
from the lips of lovely urns
where they froze on the terrible hillside

Countless as snowflakes
are the small piteous
ghosts of perpetual war

They do not need our sorrow
no thought or pity of ours
can touch them now
they are free of us

see how they move in the mist
pearly fish swimming the whiteness
infinitesimal phosphorous moons
afloat in the vapor

Starlight shines through them
into our blind eyes

EVELYN THORNE

ASSASSIN

The rattle in Trotsky's throat and his wild boar's moans.
—Piedra de Sol

Blood I foresaw. I had put by
   The distractions of the retina, the eye
That like a child must be fed and comforted
   With patterns, recognitions. The room
Had shrunk to a paperweight of glass and he
   To the centre and prisoner of its transparency.

He rasped pages. I knew too well
   The details of that head. I wiped
Clean the glance and saw
   Only his vulnerableness. Under my quivering
There was an ease, save for that starched insistence
   While paper snapped and crackled as in October air.

Sound drove out sight. We inhabited together
   One placeless cell. I must put down
This rage of the ear for discrimination, its absurd
   Dwelling on ripples, liquidities, fact
Fastening on the nerve gigantic paper burrs.
   The gate of history is straiter than eye's or ear's.

In imagination, I had driven the spike
   Down and through. The skull had sagged in its blood.
The grip, the glance—stained but firm—
   Held all at its proper distance and now hold
This autumnal hallucination of white leaves
   From burying purpose in a storm of sibilance.

I strike. I am the future and my blow
   Will have it now. If lightning froze
It would hover as here, the room
   Riding in the crest of the moment's wave,
In the deed's time, the deed's transfiguration
   And as if that wave would never again recede.

The blood wells. Prepared for this
   This I can bear. But papers
Snow to the ground with a whispered roar:
   The voice, cleaving their crescendo, is his
Voice, and his the animal cry
   That has me then by the roots of the hair.

Fleshed in that sound, objects betray me,
   Objects are my judge: the table and its shadow,
Desk and chair, the ground a pressure
   Telling me where it is that I stand
Before wall and window-light:
   Mesh of the curtain, wood, metal, flesh:

A dying body that refuses death,
   He lurches against me in his warmth and weight,
As if my arm's length blow
   Had transmitted and spent its strength
Through blood and bone; and I, spectred,
   The body that rose against me were my own.

Woven from the hair of that bent head,
   The thread that I had grasped unlabyrinthed all—
Tightrope of history and necessity—
   But the weight of a world unsteadies my feet
And I fall into the lime and contaminations
   Of contingency; into hands, looks, time.

CHARLES TOMLINSON

SUFFOLK STALLION

Sun bowled up over the reservoir water
Like a Chinaman laughing. The lanes splintered
In light, redfern and close bramble leaf,
Bird-wing and the metal case of beetle,
When the stallion came marching through
Dogroses and honeysuckle, shouldering
Dawn back over the horizon. Firestone
He crackled horseshoes on the flint lane,
Spinning pebbles into the ditches and frog homes
By the proud lift of his feathered feet.
The low air where the hedgehog went was surfed
By his polished fetlocks ringed with bunting.
Leaves freckled in the burnishing
Of the brass plates guarding his square chest
And the mighty leather of his marriage harness.
Shadow of him fell like a cardboard cut-out
On the clipped roadside hedges and, passing,
He turned their green light to darkness.

Here he comes in his massed nuptial ribbons,
His eyes rolling his burning desire,
His wide neck arched with cardinal pride,
Crashing into nature like Bucephalus
The battle behind him. And before?
His wedding in the lone meadow,
His mare waiting impatiently
His superb covering.

He passes in splendour, emboldening the birds
In their dawnsong to see him go so royally,
Square-limbed over earth, majestic haunches
Enveloped on his mighty seed.

JAMES TURNER

LYRICS FROM AUDUBON: A VISION

1.
October: and the bear,
Daft in the honey-light, yawns.

The bear's tongue, pink as a baby's, crisps to the curled tip,
It bleeds the black blood of the blueberry.

The teeth are more importantly white
Than has ever been imagined.

The bear feels his own fat
Sweeten, like a drowse, deep to the bone.

Bemused, above the fume of ruined blueberries,
The last bee hums.

The wings, like mica,
Glint in the sunlight.

He leans on his gun. Thinks
How thin is the membrane between himself and the world.

2.
In this season the waters shrink.

The spring is circular and surrounded by gold leaves
Which are fallen from the beech tree.

Not even a skitter-bug disturbs the gloss
Of the surface tension. The sky

Is reflected below in absolute clarity.
If you stare into the water you may know

That nothing disturbs the infinite blue of the sky.

3.

Listen! Stand very still and,
Far off, where shadow
Is undappled, you may hear

The tushed boar grumble in his ivy-slick.

Afterward, there is silence until
The jay, sudden as conscience, calls.

His call, in the infinite sunlight, is like
The thrill of the taste of—on the tongue—brass.

4.

For everything there is a season.

But there is a dream
Of a season past all seasons.

In such a dream the wild-grape cluster.
High-hung, exposed in the gold light,
Unripening, ripens.

Stained, the lip with wetness gleams.

I see your lip, undrying, gleam in the bright wind.

I cannot hear the sound of that wind.

ROBERT PENN WARREN

THE WINTER OF OUR DISCONTENT

Each day the earlier dark,
Each dark the strengthened cold.
Blame the fat Utility, blame rich Oil,
Blame the Old,

Those profiteers of winter.

Say, "Thou hast played most foully for it—
For Glamis, Cawdor, all."
Say the sun is rigged, and the jet-stream.
Blast City Hall,

Kiddo.

Confront, refute, confound, conspire,
And in your turn shake a leg
To convert the cold to profit,
The dark to a nest egg.

Yes, my America,

For each green fang and claw
Let the season's loot be spread,
As each day the winter widens,
And rude sons strike rude fathers

Dead.

REED WHITTEMORE

THE AGENT

Behind his back, the first wave passes over
The city which at dawn he left for good,
His staff-car musing through the streets, its tires
Kissing the rainy cheeks of cobblestones,
Till at St. Basil's gate the tower clock
Roused with a groan, flung down the hour, and shook
The tears into his eyes. In those lapped roars
And souring resonance he heard as well
Hoarse trains that highball down the world's ravines,
Some boat-horn's whoop and shudder, all sick thrills
Of transit and forsaking. Now he is calm,
Here in this locust-copse, his rendezvous,
Laying his uniform away in leaves
For good, and lacing up a peasant jerkin.
The sky fills with a suave bombination
Of yet more planes in level swarm; the city
Rocks now with flash and thud; the guildhall windows
Blink him a leaden message, that the small
Park, with its fountains, where his custom was
To sip a *fine* and watch the *passeggiata,*
Is deep in rubble and its trees afire.
But still he looks away, less now from grief
Than from a fuddled lostness how unlike
The buoyant spirits of his coming, when,
Light as a milkweed-puff, his parachute
Fell swaying toward a flashlight in a field
Of moonlit grain, which softly hove to meet him.
Bedded that night amongst the bins and kegs
Of a damp cellar, he did not rehearse

His orders, or the fear that some small flaw
In his forged self or papers might betray him,
But lay rejoicing in the smell of roots
And age, as in a painted cart next morning,
Hid under hay, he listened to the ching
Of harness and the sound of rim-struck stones.
And then that train-ride!—all compartments filled
With folk returning from the holiday,
From bonfire-jumping, dancing in a round,
And tying amulets of mistletoe.
Like some collector steeped in catalogues
Who finds at last in some dim shop or attic
A Martinique tête-bêche imperforate
Or still unbroken egg by Fabergé,
He took possession, prizing the foreknown
Half-Tartar eyes, the slurring of the schwa,
The braids and lederhosen, and the near-
Telepathy of shrugs and eyebrow-cockings
In which the nuance of their speeches lay.
Rocked by the train, with festal smiles about him,
His belly warmed by proffered *akvavit,*
He felt his hands fill with authentic gestures:
He would not shift his fork from left to right,
Nor bless himself right-shoulder-foremost. Born
Not of a culture but a drafty state,
And having, therefore, little to unlearn,
He would put on with ease the tribal ways
And ritual demeanors of this land
Toward whose chief city he was chugging now
To savor and betray.

But now a torn
Blare, like the clearing of a monstrous throat,
Rolls from those fields which vanish toward the border;
Dark tanks and halftracks come, breasting the wheat,
And after them, in combat scatterment,
Dark infantry. He can already spy
Their cold familiar eyes, their bodies heavy
With the bulk foods of home, and so remembers
A gravel playground full of lonely wind,
The warmth of a wet bed. How hard it is,
He thinks, to be cheated of a fated life
In a deep *patria,* and so to be
A foundling never lost, a pure impostor
Faithless to everything. An ill thought strikes him:
What if these soldiers, through some chance or blunder,
Have not been briefed about him and his mission?
What will they make of him—a nervous man
In farmer's costume, speaking a precious accent,
Who cannot name the streets of his own town?
Would they not, after all, be right to shoot him?
He shrinks against a trunk and waits to see.

RICHARD WILBUR

FOR DUDLEY

Even when death has taken
An exceptional man,
It is common things which touch us, gathered
In the house that proved a hostel.

Though on his desk there lie
The half of a sentence
Not to be finished by us, who lack
His gaiety, his Greek,

It is the straight back
Of a good woman
Which now we notice. For her guests' hunger
She sets the polished table.

And now the quick sun,
Rounding the gable,
Picks out a chair, a vase of flowers,
Which had stood till then in shadow.

It is the light of which
Achilles spoke,
Himself a shadow then, recalling
The splendor of mere being.

As if we were perceived
From a black ship—
A small knot of island folk,
The Light-Dwellers, pouring

A life to the dark sea—
All that we do
Is touched with ocean, yet we remain
On the shore of what we know.

We say that we are behaving
As he would have us—
He who was brave and loved this world,
Who did not hold with weeping,

Yet in the mind as in
The shut closet
Where his coats hang in black procession,
There is a covert muster.

One is moved to turn to him,
The exceptional man,
Telling him all these things, and waiting
For the deft, lucid answer.

At the sound of that voice's deep
Specific silence,
The sun winks and fails in the window.
Light perpetual keep him.

RICHARD WILBUR

SUNDAY BREWERYWORKS

The derricks lumber
    against a horizon
    that denies the stars and a yearling
    moon; this is a day the angels
fall, like wax,
        catching their skirts,
        losing their hair and nails;
    their shadows slip spread-eagled
        along the sides of buildings.

barges sleep around the bends,
    in the swamps, up in the hedges
    with the chickens. . .
the bridge stands, as it would
    if there were no river, a
    proposition;
across the water only a trolley
        carrying people.
    empty shops
    reflect and glisten.

on this bank the foliage
    grows into our laps and sighs;
    behind us the lions doze
sated through centuries of afternoons;
        derricks predicate themselves—
        there is no smoke,
            there are no whistles. . .

if we could walk across the
soggy plains
to Amsterdam,
mulch and potato rich,
if we could speak to the cows,
tear the clouds,
the sun that slaps our faces,
stuck to windmills. . .

if we could cross the water,
cross to those streets,
leafy and cold,
there we'd find a virgin
kneeling in the skirts of the Holy Ghost,
kneeling on stone,
her prayers rising to his smoke
and slatted head,
her heart,
wax pressed to chalk,
vinegar
dripping into a spoon.

PETER WILD

THE IMMORTALIST

If you were to shadow him in and out of life,
his life, day after day, you would be struck to find
that he finishes nothing. Find a coffee cup
he has drunk from; cold coffee, a half-inch of it,
sits in the bottom of the cup. The chances are
some time has passed since he poured it; wonderful plants
proliferate out of the black; alive gray spores
suck up the drink and lie hideously awake.

In his kitchen, bedroom, bathroom, and living room
—wherever there are ashtrays of whatever shapes—
hardly smoked cigarettes collect, some of them burnt
tip to tip leaving the bare ash solemn and whole
like molted fire-dragons from a Chinese egg,
the rest half-wasted, balanced on a rim of glass,
inside the paper collar their last heat hunched in.
He smokes endlessly, yet he scarcely smokes at all.

He has women. You can walk the streets anywhere
and figure to yourself that half the girls you meet
were, one time, his, all in the special way he has—
which is not quite to possess them, but to make threats
in a language indistinguishable from love's
and in gestures any woman recognizes
until it is too late for her to tell him *yes.*
By then he is not listening; then he is gone.

Everything. Everything. The same arrest, the same
disjunction, the same *no.* You cannot understand
why he reads books only part-through, and will not stay
to the end of movies; the inside record grooves
of his collection are unworn, he has not learned
a single poem by heart, he does not eat desserts.
You wonder who *he* is, never to finish with—
and, if this pleases him, what he will not come to. . . .

ROBLEY WILSON, JR.

THE SLEEPWALKER

Someone I sleep with rises,
walks down a hall
in dark thick as held breath.
He feels down the stairs,
eases the latch into the street.
Wind lights swing.
Stars arch a vague spine.

There he begins to form.
His face struggles out of flesh,
and his name hardens his tongue.
Small creatures in holes, in tunnels,
in the thatch of weeds,
lift their ears in his fingertips,
and his palms breathe.

it is one night given
Around him, the houses open
in his eyes, doors, walls,
blankets and sheets.
He enters all dreams at once:
a king for the mailed prince,
a dead brother forgiving,
falling back in blood,
for those who sleep with weapons.
His kiss cools on new breasts,
and children turn and turn
in the fur of their dreams.

On a curled country road
where the field shakes loose,
where the shack wood spirals from paint,
a billboard peels its decades;
each bright, accessible image
flowers, sickens, falls
back through the wars, depressions,
until the screen stutters black.
Then, in the boards,
whorls contract, drawing the wood back
into boles, into seeds.

all things yield their names
When someone I sleep with walks
into dreams that dream us,
become us when we lay down our watches,
our wallets. When someone
I walk with sleeps, all things
spin dark, and sigh loose the light
we close into our lives.

He turns, the dawn vague on his face,
to climb up to waking.
The clock's spiral nebula fades,
the hammer trembles.
He climbs down into my sleep.

I know I won't remember again,
as I strap on my names.
No wake of dreams will follow me out.
I will drive into the billboards
I have chosen to live for.

JOHN WOODS